# RISING STARS
## Maths

# Fluency with Fractions

## TEACHER'S GUIDE

### Steph King

## YEAR
# 3

**Rising Stars UK Ltd**
**7 Hatchers Mews, Bermondsey Street, London, SE1 3GS**

**www.risingstars-uk.com**

Every effort has been made to trace copyright holders and obtain their permission for the use of copyright materials. The authors and publisher will gladly receive information enabling them to rectify any error or omission in subsequent editions. All facts are correct at time of going to press.

Published 2014
Reprinted 2014, 2015
Text, design and layout © Rising Stars UK Ltd.

**Author:** Steph King
**Consultant:** Cherri Moseley
**Publisher:** Fiona Lazenby
**Project Manager:** Debbie Allen
**Editorial:** Katharine Timberlake, Kate Manson
**Cover design:** Burville-Riley Partnership
**Design:** Marc Burville-Riley
**Typesetting:** Fakenham Prepress Solutions
**Illustrations:** Louise Forshaw / Advocate Art, Richard and Benjamin,
    Fakenham Prepress Solutions
**CD-ROM development:** Alex Morris

British Library Cataloguing in Publication Data.
A CIP record for this book is available from the British Library.

ISBN: 978-1-78339-182-0

Printed by: Ashford Colour Press Ltd, Gosport, Hants

# Contents

## Fractions in the 2014 National Curriculum

The National Curriculum aims to ensure that all pupils become fluent in the fundamentals of mathematics, can reason mathematically and can solve problems by applying their mathematics. With a significant shift in expectations in the 2014 Programme of Study, children are required to work with and calculate using a range of fractions at an earlier stage. Achieving fluency will depend on developing conceptual understanding through a variety of practical and contextual opportunities.

## Statutory requirements and non-statutory guidance

At first glance, the statutory requirements for the Fractions domain for younger children may not appear to be that extensive. However, it is important to note that each 'objective' is made up of a range of different skills and knowledge that need to be addressed. We must remember that mastery of one aspect does not necessarily imply mastery of another.

The Programme of Study also provides non-statutory guidance that helps to clarify, secure and extend learning in each domain to best prepare children for the next stage of mathematical development. Units in this *Fluency with Fractions* series, therefore, also address some aspects of the non-statutory guidance. These objectives are flagged where applicable.

## Fractions across the domains

Learning about fractions is not exclusive to the Fractions domain in the Programme of Study. Conceptual understanding of fractions is also addressed and applied through work on time, turns, angles and through many other aspects of measurement, geometry and also statistics. We must also remember to continue to practise and extend learning from previous year groups even if a concept is not explicitly covered in the Programme of Study for the current year group. The other domains provide useful opportunities for this.

## Making the links: decimals, percentages, ratio and proportion

Children will first experience decimals in the context of measurement. However, security with place value is vital if they are to truly understand how the position of a digit on either side of the decimal point determines its size. Place value charts and grids are used in this series of books to continue to reinforce this concept and to help children make sense of tenths, hundredths and thousandths.

As children progress through the Programmes of Study, they will later meet percentages. Recognising that a fraction such as $\frac{25}{100}$ can be written as $25 \div 100$, and therefore as 0.25, will help make the connection to 25%.

Finding and identifying equivalent fractions will later pave the way for understanding equivalent ratios.

For this reason, within the *Fluency with Fractions* series, the Year 4 book includes work on decimals, Year 5 includes percentages and Year 6 goes on to incorporate ratio and proportion.

## Developing conceptual understanding through the use of resources

Children should be given opportunities to develop conceptual understanding through a range of practical experiences and the use of visual representations to help them make sense of fractions. Manipulatives, such as Base 10 apparatus, cubes and counters, along with other resources, should be used skilfully to model concepts and provide a reference point to help children make connections for future learning. Moving in this way from concrete resources to pictorial representations to symbolic notation for fractions will help to secure conceptual understanding.

## Developing mathematical language

Language is often cited as a barrier to learning, so it is important to model technical vocabulary that helps children to use it confidently and to help them explain their mathematical thinking and reasoning. Appropriate language structures are suggested throughout the Units.

# Using representations to support understanding

Fractions is a part of mathematics that children often find more difficult to learn than other areas. This, in turn, is often the result of teachers finding the concepts more difficult to teach. We need to help children to see what we mean and make links to other familiar representations that they know, e.g. number lines.

Historically, images to support the teaching of fractions have tended to be related to real-life examples that children see 'cut-up' and shared. Pizzas, cakes and chocolate are examples of this. Although these representations are valuable (particularly circular images that will later inform work on pie charts), it is the linear image that directly relates to the number line that will support the transition of concrete to abstract when counting and calculating.

Throughout the *Fluency with Fractions* resources, fraction bar images are used in each year level to introduce the concept of fractions as equal parts of a whole, equivalence, counting (linked to the number line) and calculating.

The following diagrams provide a few generic examples to illustrate how different images are used. Templates for some useful images are provided on the accompanying CD-ROM.

- Fractions as equal parts of one whole.

- Linking fractions to counting on a number line.

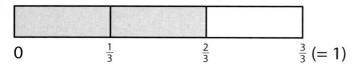

- Counting on the number line to reinforce that fractions are numbers in their own right. Counting paves the way for calculating.

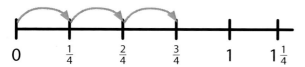

- Developing a range of images to explore equivalent fractions.

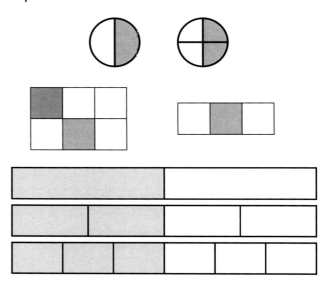

- Comparing fractions on a number line.

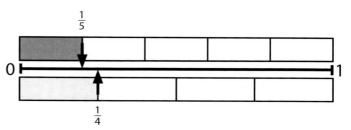

- Using fraction bars to support early calculation of fractions of amounts.

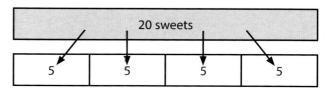

- Using fraction bars to support identifying an amount represented by a fraction.

# How to use this book

The Units in this book support the development of conceptual understanding of fractions and are intended to be used to introduce concepts. Learning should be practised and revisited regularly using other resources to consolidate and deepen understanding.

Each Unit within the books is structured in the same way, providing guidance to support teachers and an example teaching sequence.

Tasks can be used as suggested or adapted accordingly to meet the needs of each setting. Guided learning provides an opportunity for the adult to take learning forward with a group or to take part in an activity that has a greater problem-solving element and where language may be more demanding. Additional editable resource sheets are provided on the accompanying CD-ROM to support this.

Bold text shows the link to the NC objectives or the non-statutory guidance.

Please check that prior learning is in place before working on this unit.

This section helps teachers to make connections through the use of visual representations and language structures.

Tasks may be directed at the teacher to run the activity with children as guided learning; directed at the teacher to explain the activity to children to do independently; or directed at children to be photocopied and given out for independent work. Tasks increase in level of difficulty.

Task B is aimed at the majority of children who will progress at the expected rate.

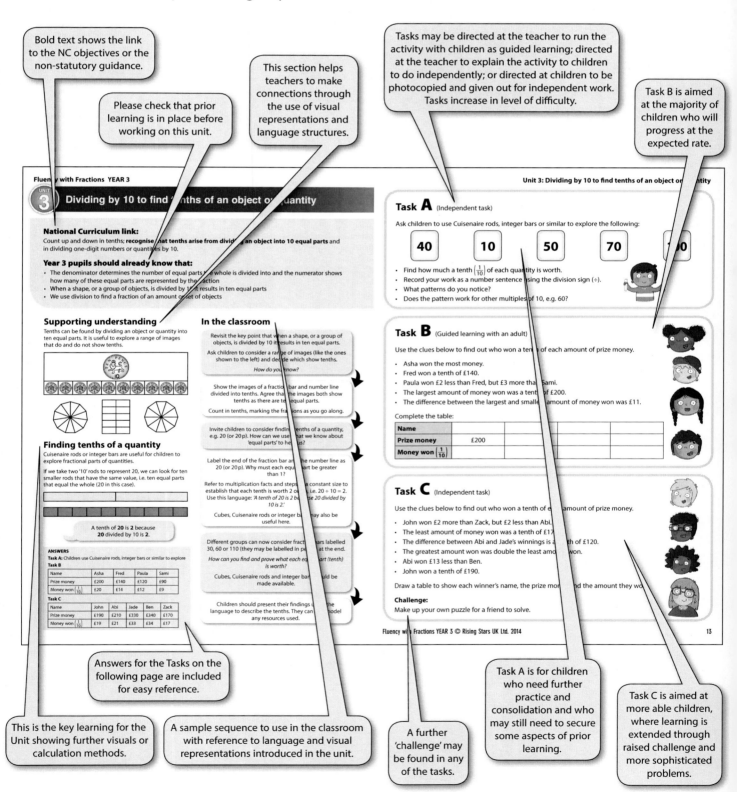

Answers for the Tasks on the following page are included for easy reference.

This is the key learning for the Unit showing further visuals or calculation methods.

A sample sequence to use in the classroom with reference to language and visual representations introduced in the unit.

A further 'challenge' may be found in any of the tasks.

Task A is for children who need further practice and consolidation and who may still need to secure some aspects of prior learning.

Task C is aimed at more able children, where learning is extended through raised challenge and more sophisticated problems.

# Curriculum mapping grid

The grid below shows in which Units objectives from the 2014 National Curriculum Programme of Study for Year 3 are covered. Note that objectives are revisited regularly and learning progressed in subsequent units. In the National Curriculum link section of each Unit, bold text is used to indicate which specific part of the overarching objective is addressed within the Unit, since objectives often cover a range of different knowledge and skills (particularly for younger age groups).

| Objectives | Unit | | | | | | | | | | | | | | | | | | | | | |
|---|---|---|---|---|---|---|---|---|---|---|---|---|---|---|---|---|---|---|---|---|---|---|
| | 1 | 2 | 3 | 4 | 5 | 6 | 7 | 8 | 9 | 10 | 11 | 12 | 13 | 14 | 15 | 16 | 17 | 18 | 19 | 20 | 21 | 22 |
| Recognise and use fractions as numbers: unit fractions and non-unit fractions with small denominators. | ✔ | ✔ | | | | | | | | | | | | | | | | | | | | |
| Count up and down in tenths; recognise that tenths arise from dividing an object into 10 equal parts and in dividing one-digit numbers or quantities by 10. | | | ✔ | ✔ | ✔ | ✔ | | | | | | | | | | | | | | | | |
| Compare and order unit fractions, and fractions with the same denominators. | | | | | | | ✔ | ✔ | | | | | | | | | | | | | | |
| Recognise, find and write fractions of a discrete set of objects: unit fractions and non-unit fractions with small denominators. | | | | | | | | | ✔ | ✔ | ✔ | | | | | | | | | | | |
| Add and subtract fractions with the same denominator within one whole [for example $\frac{5}{7} + \frac{1}{7} = \frac{6}{7}$]. | | | | | | | | | | | | ✔ | ✔ | ✔ | ✔ | ✔ | | | | | | |
| Recognise and show, using diagrams, equivalent fractions with small denominators. | | | | | | | | | | | | | | | | | ✔ | ✔ | | | ✔ | ✔ |
| Understand the relation between unit fractions as operators (fractions of), and division by integers. | | | | | | | | | | | | | | | | | | | ✔ | ✔ | | |

# UNIT 1

# Fractions as numbers (1)

## National Curriculum link:

**Recognise and use fractions as numbers: unit fractions and non-unit fractions with small denominators.**

## Year 3 pupils should already know that:

- A fraction is a number in its own right
- All fractions can be placed on the number line
- The denominator determines the number of equal parts the whole is divided into and the numerator shows how many of these equal parts are represented by the fraction

## Supporting understanding

Depending on children's experience, it is possible that fractions have predominantly been represented as parts of shapes.

The 2014 requirements in Year 2 should mean that this is no longer the case, however, as the non-statutory guidance provides examples of counting in fraction steps of quarters or halves up to 10.

Exploring folding strips of paper of the same length to show halves, quarters, eighths, etc. helps to secure understanding. These strips can represent a number line from 0 to 1 where each fold becomes a labelled position on the line:

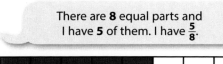

$$0 \qquad \frac{1}{4} \qquad \frac{2}{4} \qquad \frac{3}{4} \qquad \frac{4}{4} (= 1)$$

Additional strips can be added to show fractions greater than 1. Children should count in fraction steps beyond 1.

## Non-unit fractions

Language structures, such as the example shown here, can support children to make sense of the fractions they are working with.

> There are **8** equal parts and I have **5** of them. I have $\frac{5}{8}$.

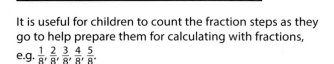

It is useful for children to count the fraction steps as they go to help prepare them for calculating with fractions, e.g. $\frac{1}{8}, \frac{2}{8}, \frac{3}{8}, \frac{4}{8}, \frac{5}{8}$.

### ANSWERS

**Task A:** Children make fractions **Task B: 3)** Example: *'There are 4 equal parts and I have 3 of them. I have $\frac{3}{4}$.'* **Task C:** Examples:
**1)** Sami has $\frac{6}{6}, \frac{6}{7}, \frac{6}{8}$, etc. so the others must have a fraction that is smaller, e.g. Tony $\frac{5}{8}$ **2)** E.g. Sami $\frac{6}{8}$, Tony $\frac{3}{8}$ and Jade $\frac{2}{8} \left(\frac{1}{4}\right)$
**3)** Sami $\frac{6}{24}$ and Jade $\frac{1}{4}$ **4)** Sami $\frac{6}{12}$ and Tony $\frac{4}{8}$ **5)** $\frac{2}{8}, \frac{3}{12}, \frac{4}{16}$, etc.

## In the classroom

Revisit the key point that the denominator determines the number of equal parts the whole is divided into.

Use the example that when we find a half we divide by two to create two equal parts.
Show talking point images with correct and incorrect representations of wholes divided into parts, e.g.

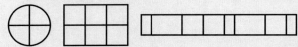

Invite children to explain how they know which images are correct and which are not. Use language such as:
*'I know that the image does not show eighths because the eight parts are not all equal.'*

Ask children to consider ways to ensure that there are eight equal parts. Children should practise folding paper strips in half, half again and half again. Encourage them to describe the fractions that are represented after each fold. Count in eighths along the strip. Introduce the term 'non-unit fraction'.

Pose these, or similar, questions for different groups to consider:

- *How many eighths are there altogether in the whole? Practise counting them from zero to one and back again.*

- *I'm thinking of a fraction that can be shown using our strip. I counted an odd number of eighths. What could my fraction be? What couldn't it be?*

- *How many eighths are there altogether in two wholes? In three wholes? How do you know?*

- *How could you use what you know about folding the strip into eighths to help create a correct image for sixths? Have a go.*

Finally, consider the notation of a non-unit fraction, e.g. $\frac{5}{8}$ or $\frac{5}{6}$. Show these fractions shaded on strips (or covered by counters) and the language structure, e.g.
*'There are eight equal parts and I have five of them. I have $\frac{5}{8}$.'*
Get children to practise using the language for another fraction on their strip.

# Task **A** (Independent task)

| | | | |
|---|---|---|---|

| | | | | | | | |
|---|---|---|---|---|---|---|---|

**1)** Roll the dice.

**2)** Choose to cover this number of parts with counters on the quarters or eighths strip.

**3)** Count the parts covered in fraction steps.

**4)** Write down the fraction you have made.

**5)** Roll again.

Example:
- I roll a 3 and choose to use the eighths strip.
- I cover three parts of my strip with counters.
- I count 1 eighth, 2 eighths, 3 eighths and then write the fraction $\frac{3}{8}$.

# Task **B** (Independent task)

**1)** Make a fraction strip by folding to show quarters. Label the folds to show $\frac{1}{4}$, $\frac{2}{4}$ and $\frac{3}{4}$. Make another strip by folding to show eighths. Label the folds.

**2)** Use your 'quarters' strip or your 'eighths' strip to find these fractions and describe them using the language in the speech bubble. Use counters to help you show how many quarters or eighths there are each time.

$$\frac{3}{8} \qquad \frac{1}{4} \qquad \frac{4}{8} \qquad \frac{2}{4} \qquad \frac{7}{8} \qquad \frac{3}{4} \qquad \frac{6}{8}$$

There are ___ equal parts and I have ___ of them. I have ___.

**3)** Choose two of the fractions and write what you have found out in a speech bubble.

# Task **C** (Independent or guided learning with an adult)

There are ___ equal parts and I have **6** of them. I have ___.

**Sami**

There are **8** equal parts and I have ___ of them. I have ___.

**Tony**

There are ___ equal parts and I have ___ of them. I have $\frac{1}{4}$.

**Jade**

Use the information and paper strips to find fractions for Sami, Tony and Jade so that:

**1)** Sami has the largest fraction of his strip shaded this time.

**2)** Tony has less than Sami, but more than Jade shaded on his strip.

**3)** Sami and Jade have the same amount shaded.

**4)** Tony and Sami both have half of their strips shaded.

**5)** Jade has more than four equal parts in her strip. Find at least two possible solutions.

# UNIT 2
# Fractions as numbers (2)

## National Curriculum link:

**Recognise and use fractions as numbers: unit fractions and non-unit fractions with small denominators.**

## Year 3 pupils should already know that:

- A fraction is a number in its own right
- All fractions can be placed on the number line
- The denominator determines the number of equal parts the whole is divided into and the numerator shows how many of these equal parts are represented by the fraction

## Supporting understanding

In Unit 1, children explored fractions such as quarters and eighths on paper strips to help secure their understanding of unit and non-unit fractions as numbers on the number line.

Other fractions, such as thirds and sixths, tenths and fifths, can be explored in a similar way.

There are **3** equal parts and I have **2** of them. I have $\frac{2}{3}$.

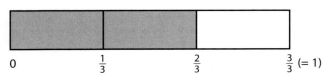

0          $\frac{1}{3}$          $\frac{2}{3}$          $\frac{3}{3}$ (= 1)

## Fractions on the number line

These fractions can also be shown on the number line to reinforce that they are numbers. We can show this as fraction steps.

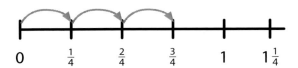

0     $\frac{1}{4}$     $\frac{2}{4}$     $\frac{3}{4}$     1     $1\frac{1}{4}$

Each step has a value of $\frac{1}{4}$.

Again, the language structure can be used to secure the understanding that there are four equal parts and $\frac{3}{4}$ represents three of these equal parts.

**ANSWERS**
**Task A: 1)** $\frac{3}{4}$ **2)** $\frac{1}{3}$ **3)** $\frac{2}{3}$ **4)** $\frac{2}{5}$ **5)** Number line with 4 steps of a fifth **Task B:** A selection of number lines with fraction steps for fractions such as $\frac{3}{4}$, $\frac{3}{5}$, $\frac{4}{10}$, etc. **Challenge: 1)** E.g. $\frac{3}{3}$, $\frac{4}{4}$, $\frac{5}{5}$, etc. or $\frac{7}{8}$ or $\frac{9}{10}$ (if 9 chosen for the question mark) **2)** $\frac{3}{6}$, $\frac{4}{8}$, $\frac{5}{10}$ or $\frac{2}{4}$ (if 2 chosen for question mark **3)** $\frac{1}{10}$ **Task C:** A selection of number lines with fraction steps for fractions such as $\frac{3}{5}$, $\frac{4}{9}$, $\frac{7}{10}$, etc.
**1)** E.g. $\frac{5}{5}$ or $\frac{7}{8}$ or children's use of the question marks **2)** $\frac{2}{6}$ and $\frac{3}{9}$ or children's use of the question marks **3)** $\frac{2}{10}$ or children's use of the question marks **4)** E.g. $\frac{7}{6}$ as $1\frac{1}{6}$

## In the classroom

Invite children to rehearse the language used in Unit 1 to describe unit and non-unit fractions.

Provide differentiated images for children to describe.

Model the use of a number line to show the key point that fractions are numbers in their own right, e.g. $\frac{5}{8}$.

Count in eighths and use this language: *There are … equal parts and I have … of them. I have …* to secure understanding. Count beyond one as '$1\frac{1}{8}$, $1\frac{2}{8}$' etc.

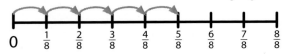

0     $\frac{1}{8}$     $\frac{2}{8}$     $\frac{3}{8}$     $\frac{4}{8}$     $\frac{5}{8}$     $\frac{6}{8}$     $\frac{7}{8}$     $\frac{8}{8}$

Invite children to draw similar number lines to represent the images they were describing previously.

Encourage them to count and use the language above.

Pose these, or similar, questions for different groups to consider about their own number lines:

- *How many fraction steps have you counted?*
- *How many more do you need to count to reach 1?*
- *Is your fraction larger or smaller than $\frac{1}{2}$? How do you know?*
- *How many more do you need to count to reach a number beyond 1?*

Present the following problem:

Jade made three fraction steps along her number line.

- What fraction could this be? *'It could be … because …'*
- What fraction couldn't this be? *'It couldn't be … because …'*

Record some of the suggestions for the possible fraction, e.g. $\frac{3}{3}$, $\frac{3}{4}$, $\frac{3}{5}$, $\frac{3}{6}$, $\frac{3}{7}$, etc. and ask different groups to consider the following ideas:

- *Which of these fractions is equal to or nearest to 1?*
- *Which of these fractions is equal to or nearest to a half?*
- *Which is the smallest fraction and will be closest to 0?*

# Task **A** (Independent task)

Use the language 'There are ___ equal parts and I have ___ of them. I have ___ ' to help describe the fraction on each number line. Write down the fraction.

1)

2)

3)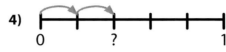

4)

**5)** Draw your own number line for the fraction $\frac{4}{5}$.

# Task **B** (Independent task or guided learning with an adult)

- Thinking carefully, choose a number for the numerator and another for the denominator to make at least five fractions.
- Use the language 'There are ___ equal parts and I have ___ of them. I have ___ ' to describe each fraction.
- Draw the number line to match each fraction.
- Make another fraction. Use the '**?**' as a numerator greater than 1 of your choice.

**Challenge:**

**1)** Which of your fractions is equal to 1 or nearest to 1?

**2)** Are any of your fractions equal to a half? Which ones?

**3)** Which is the smallest fraction and will be closest to 0?

| Numerators | | |
|---|---|---|
| 1 | 3 | 4 |
| 5 | 7 | ? |
| Denominators | | |
| 3 | 4 | 5 |
| 6 | 8 | 10 |

# Task **C** (Independent task)

- Thinking carefully, choose a number for the numerator and another for the denominator to make at least five fractions.
- Use the language 'There are ___ equal parts and I have ___ of them. I have ___ ' to describe each fraction.
- Draw the number line to match each fraction.
- Make another fraction. Use the '**?**' for a numerator or denominator greater than 1 of your choice.

**1)** Which of your fractions is equal to 1 or nearest to 1?

**2)** Are any of your fractions equal to a third?

**3)** Which is the smallest fraction and will be closest to 0?

**4)** Can you make a fraction that is greater than 1?

| Numerators | | |
|---|---|---|
| 2 | 3 | 4 |
| 5 | 7 | ? |
| Denominators | | |
| 5 | 6 | 8 |
| 9 | 10 | ? |

# UNIT 3  Dividing by 10 to find tenths of an object or quantity

## National Curriculum link:

Count up and down in tenths; **recognise that tenths arise from dividing an object into 10 equal parts** and in dividing one-digit numbers or quantities by 10.

## Year 3 pupils should already know that:

- The denominator determines the number of equal parts the whole is divided into and the numerator shows how many of these equal parts are represented by the fraction
- When a shape, or a group of objects, is divided by 10 it results in ten equal parts
- We use division to find a fraction of an amount or set of objects

## Supporting understanding

Tenths can be found by dividing an object or quantity into ten equal parts. It is useful to explore a range of images that do and do not show tenths.

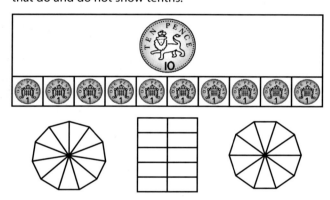

## Finding tenths of a quantity

Cuisenaire rods or integer bars are useful for children to explore fractional parts of quantities.

If we take two '10' rods to represent 20, we can look for ten smaller rods that have the same value, i.e. ten equal parts that equal the whole (20 in this case).

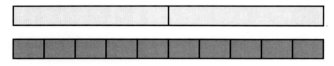

A tenth of **20** is **2** because
**20** divided by 10 is **2**.

## In the classroom

Revisit the key point that when a shape, or a group of objects, is divided by 10 it results in ten equal parts.

Ask children to consider a range of images (like the ones shown to the left) and decide which show tenths.

*How do you know?*

Show the images of a fraction bar and number line divided into tenths. Agree that the images both show tenths as there are ten equal parts.

Count in tenths, marking the fractions as you go along.

Invite children to consider finding tenths of a quantity, e.g. 20 (or 20 p). How can we use what we know about 'equal parts' to help us?

Label the end of the fraction bar and the number line as 20 (or 20 p). Why must each equal part be greater than 1?

Refer to multiplication facts and steps of a constant size to establish that each tenth is worth 2 or 2 p, i.e. 20 ÷ 10 = 2. Use this language: *'A tenth of 20 is 2 because 20 divided by 10 is 2.'*

Cubes, Cuisenaire rods or integer bars may also be useful here.

Different groups can now consider fraction bars labelled 30, 60 or 110 (they may be labelled in pence) at the end.

*How can you find and prove what each equal part (tenth) is worth?*

Cubes, Cuisenaire rods and integer bars should be made available.

Children should present their findings using the language to describe the tenths. They can also model any resources used.

**ANSWERS**

**Task A:** Children use Cuisenaire rods, integer bars or similar to explore

**Task B**

| Name | Asha | Fred | Paula | Sami |
|---|---|---|---|---|
| Prize money | £200 | £140 | £120 | £90 |
| Money won $\left(\frac{1}{10}\right)$ | £20 | £14 | £12 | £9 |

**Task C**

| Name | John | Abi | Jade | Ben | Zack |
|---|---|---|---|---|---|
| Prize money | £190 | £210 | £330 | £340 | £170 |
| Money won $\left(\frac{1}{10}\right)$ | £19 | £21 | £33 | £34 | £17 |

# Task A (Independent task)

Ask children to use Cuisenaire rods, integer bars or similar to explore the following:

| 40 | 10 | 50 | 70 | 100 |

- Find how much a tenth $\left(\frac{1}{10}\right)$ of each quantity is worth.
- Record your work as a number sentence using the division sign (÷).
- What patterns do you notice?
- Does the pattern work for other multiples of 10, e.g. 60?

# Task B (Guided learning with an adult)

Use the clues below to find out who won a tenth of each amount of prize money.

- Asha won the most money.
- Fred won a tenth of £140.
- Paula won £2 less than Fred, but £3 more than Sami.
- The largest amount of money won was a tenth of £200.
- The difference between the largest and smallest amount of money won was £11.

Complete the table:

| Name | | | | |
|---|---|---|---|---|
| **Prize money** | £200 | | | |
| **Money won** $\left(\frac{1}{10}\right)$ | | | | |

# Task C (Independent task)

Use the clues below to find out who won a tenth of each amount of prize money.

- John won £2 more than Zack, but £2 less than Abi.
- The least amount of money won was a tenth of £170.
- The difference between Abi and Jade's winnings is a tenth of £120.
- The greatest amount won was double the least amount won.
- Abi won £13 less than Ben.
- John won a tenth of £190.

Draw a table to show each winner's name, the prize money and the amount they won.

**Challenge:**

Make up your own puzzle for a friend to solve.

# Finding tenths by dividing one-digit numbers by 10

## National Curriculum link:
Count up and down in tenths; recognise that tenths arise from dividing an object into 10 equal parts **and in dividing one-digit numbers or quantities by 10.**

## Year 3 pupils should already know that:
- When a shape, or a group of objects, is divided by 10 it results in ten equal parts
- Dividing by 10 makes a whole number 10 times smaller, e.g. 20 ÷ 10 = 2

## Supporting understanding

In Unit 3, children explored how tenths arise from dividing objects into ten equal parts and dividing quantities by 10. This unit will focus on using place value to secure understanding of tenths.

In Year 2, children relate the multiplication table of 10 to place value:

| Tens | Units or ones | |
|---|---|---|
| | 2 | |
| 2 | 0 | $2 \times 10$ |
| | 2 | $20 \div 2$ |

Knowing how place value can be used in this way provides a vital link when working with tenths and later on with hundredths, etc. This also supports understanding of decimal measure.

## Dividing a one-digit number by 10

| Units or ones | ● | tenths | |
|---|---|---|---|
| 1 | | | |
| | | 1 | $1 \div 10$ |
| 1 | | | $\frac{1}{10} \times 10$ |

Fractions relate directly to division. This means that a familiar division sentence such as 20 ÷ 10 can be written using fractional notation, i.e. $\frac{20}{10}$.

In the same way, 1 ÷ 10 can be written as $\frac{1}{10}$ and 2 ÷ 10 as $\frac{2}{10}$.

### ANSWERS
**Task A:** Children write number sentences for dividing multiples of 10 by 10, e.g. 40 ÷ 10 = 4 **Task B:** Children take a digit card and put it on the place value grid and divide the number by 10 **Challenge:** The digit card cannot be 7 as this would result in $\frac{7}{10}$ not $\frac{8}{10}$ **Task C:** Children take a 'tenths' card and write this as a fraction **Challenge:** 1 in the units column and 2 in the tenths column; 12 cannot go in the tenths column as it is more than $\frac{10}{10}$; the $\frac{10}{10}$ are equal to 1 unit

## In the classroom

Revisit the key point that dividing by 10 makes a whole number 10 times smaller.

Invite children to write down a division fact of their choice that shows a whole number made 10 times smaller.

Model an example, e.g. 30, on the place value grid, making clear the number of places and direction that the digits must move.

Agree that using place value in this way shows that 30 ÷ 10 = 3.

Children should quickly use the place value grid to check their own division facts.

Revisit the key point that when a shape, or a group of objects, is divided by 10 it results in ten equal parts.

So, 30 ÷ 10 results in ten equal parts: 10 groups of 3.

But what happens when we want to divide a number that is less than 10 by 10?

Pose these, or similar, questions for different groups to consider:
- *What can you tell me about the size of the ten equal groups?*
- *What fractions might we need to use? Why?*

Model 1 ÷ 10 on the place value grid, introducing the new column of tenths.

*So, 1 ÷ 10 results in ten equal parts or groups of $\frac{1}{10}$.*

Record in a number sentence: 1 ÷ 10 = $\frac{1}{10}$.

Use the fraction bar visual from Unit 3 to agree that tenths arise from dividing a whole into ten equal parts.

# Task A (Guided learning with an adult)

Children are still likely to need to secure dividing numbers by 10 that result in whole number answers. This underpins the lesson objective as prior learning.

Use the time to secure the division facts for the multiplication table of 10.

- You will need number cards showing multiples of 10 up to 100.
- Children should take it in turns to choose a number card.
- Write the number sentence for dividing by 10, e.g. 40 ÷ 10, and discuss the number of equal parts (or groups) that will arise from the calculation and the size of each group.
- Confirm the division fact and model using a place value grid.

| Tens | Units or ones |
|------|---------------|
| 4    | 0             |
|      | 4             |

40 ÷ 10

You will need digits cards 0 to 9 and a place value grid.

# Task B (Independent task)

1) Take a digit card and put it on the place value grid.
2) Divide the number by 10. Remember that you will need to move the digit card!
3) Record in a number sentence.
4) Repeat.

| Units or ones • | tenths |
|-----------------|--------|
|                 |        |
|                 |        |

**Challenge:**

Sami wrote: $\boxed{\phantom{0}} \div 10 = \frac{8}{10}$.

How do you know that he did not start with the digit card 7?

# Task C (Independent task)

You will need 'tenths' cards, e.g.

### 6 tenths

1) Take a 'tenths' card and write this as a fraction.
2) Write the division fact that was used to create your fraction.
3) Check using a place value grid.

**Challenge:**

Jade was playing a different game. She wrote this division fact: $12 \div 10 = \frac{12}{10}$

What would this look like on the place value grid? Draw it.

Why can Jade not put '12' in the tenths column like this?

| Tens | Units or ones • | tenths |
|------|-----------------|--------|
|      |                 | 12     |

# Counting in tenths, including beyond 1

## National Curriculum link:

**Count up and down in tenths;** recognise that tenths arise from dividing an object into 10 equal parts and in dividing one-digit numbers or quantities by 10.

## Year 3 pupils should already know that:

- All fractions can be placed on the number line
- We can count beyond 1 in fraction steps on the number line
- When a shape, or a group of objects, is divided by 10 it results in ten equal parts

## Supporting understanding

In Units 3 and 4, children recognised that tenths arise from dividing an object into ten equal parts and in dividing one-digit numbers or quantities by 10.

Children should count on and back in tenths and steps of more than one tenth, e.g. two tenths.

We can use a fraction strip or 'bar' to represent steps of tenths. A counting stick, or a metre ruler, is also useful here.

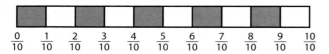

$\frac{0}{10}$  $\frac{1}{10}$  $\frac{2}{10}$  $\frac{3}{10}$  $\frac{4}{10}$  $\frac{5}{10}$  $\frac{6}{10}$  $\frac{7}{10}$  $\frac{8}{10}$  $\frac{9}{10}$  $\frac{10}{10}$

## Counting in tenths beyond 1

In Year 2, children count in fraction steps of halves and quarters up to 10.

Counting in tenths in this way will start to reinforce mixed numbers, as well as build the foundations for calculating with fractions and understanding decimal place value in Year 4, e.g. $\frac{7}{10}$ and $\frac{5}{10}$ more is $\frac{12}{10}$ or $1\frac{2}{10}$, which will also later be shown as 0.7 and 0.5 more is 1.2.

## In the classroom

Revisit the key point that the denominator determines the number of equal parts the whole is divided into.

Use the image of a 'tenths' bar to count in tenths, marking the fractions as you go along.

Practise counting on and back in tenths and in different steps of more than one tenth, e.g. $\frac{2}{10}$.
Pose questions, such as:

- *How many tenths have I counted? How do you know?*

- *How many steps of $\frac{2}{10}$ can I take to equal one whole? What related facts did you use to help you?*

- *How many tenths are equivalent to the fraction one half? One fifth? Or to two, three or ten wholes? How do you know?*

Revisit the key point that we can count in fraction steps beyond 1 on the number line. Link the 'tenths' bar used previously to the number line and ask children to consider what would happen to the number line when a second and then third 'tenths' bar is added.

Pose these, or similar, questions for different groups to consider:

- *How many tenths can we see now? How can we use this to help us predict the number of tenths in five or six bars?*

- *How many tenths are there in $1\frac{3}{10}$, in total?*

- *Can you find another way to write 15 tenths? 25 tenths?*

Establish that mixed numbers can be used to help us work with fractions greater than 1.

# Task **A** (Independent task)

**HINT:** Remember that you may need to use a second bar if you have to count past 1!

You need two 'tenths' bars, fraction cards, a counter and a dice.

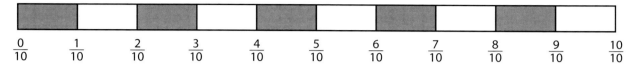

$\frac{0}{10}$ $\frac{1}{10}$ $\frac{2}{10}$ $\frac{3}{10}$ $\frac{4}{10}$ $\frac{5}{10}$ $\frac{6}{10}$ $\frac{7}{10}$ $\frac{8}{10}$ $\frac{9}{10}$ $\frac{10}{10}$

1) Label your 'tenths' bars.

2) Take a fraction card and place your counter on this fraction.

3) Roll the dice.

4) Count on (or back) this many tenths on your fraction bar.

5) Record what you have done, e.g. $\frac{3}{10}$⌒⌒⌒⌒$\frac{7}{10}$.

6) Take a new fraction card and repeat.

# Task **B** (Independent task)

You need several 'tenths' bars, fraction cards and two dice.

1) Label your 'tenths' bars.

Take it in turns to:

2) Take a fraction card and place your counter on this fraction.

3) Roll the two dice.

**HINT:** Remember that you will need to use more than one 'tenths' bar if you have to count past 1!

4) Decide which number to use for your fraction steps, e.g. use the 3 for $\frac{3}{10}$ or the 2 for $\frac{2}{10}$. The other dice tells you the number of steps to take along the bar, e.g. two steps or three steps.

5) Record your steps in your own way. Remember to use mixed numbers to help you.

6) Take a new fraction card and repeat.

# Task **C** (Independent task or guided learning with an adult)

Bob starts his count from $\frac{1}{2}$ and Asha starts her count from $\frac{1}{10}$. They stop when they count past the number 5 on the number line.

I'm counting in steps of $\frac{3}{10}$.

**Bob**

I'm counting in steps of $\frac{4}{10}$.

1) Who do you think will reach the number 5 first? Why?

2) Record the steps that each child makes. Remember to use mixed numbers to help you.

3) Which fractions do both children land on in their count?

4) Will either child land exactly on the number 7? How do you know?

**Asha**

**UNIT 6**

# Using knowledge of tenths

## National Curriculum link:

**Count up and down in tenths; recognise that tenths arise from dividing an object into 10 equal parts and in dividing one-digit numbers or quantities by 10.**

## Year 3 pupils should already know that:

- All fractions can be placed on the number line
- When a shape, or a group of objects, is divided by 10 it results in ten equal parts
- We can count on and back in fraction steps on the number line
- There are 100 cm in a metre

## Supporting understanding

In Unit 5, children counted on and back in steps of a tenth on fraction bars and on the number line.

It is useful to make links to other areas of mathematics to help provide a purpose and context, as well as supporting future work on decimals.

Consider a metre stick and steps of a tenth.

Use knowledge of a metre to determine the value of each tenth, i.e. 10 cm.

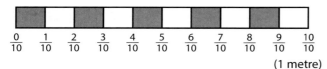

$\frac{0}{10}$ $\frac{1}{10}$ $\frac{2}{10}$ $\frac{3}{10}$ $\frac{4}{10}$ $\frac{5}{10}$ $\frac{6}{10}$ $\frac{7}{10}$ $\frac{8}{10}$ $\frac{9}{10}$ $\frac{10}{10}$

(1 metre)

## Other opportunities to consider tenths in measurement

Linking tenths to money will support decimal place value and use of the pound (£) notation, e.g. £1.20, where 20 p is worth $\frac{2}{10}$ of a pound.

Fraction bars can be used to show fractional equivalents of one pound.

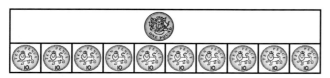

### ANSWERS

**Task A:** Children label the metre strip **Task B: 1)** 3 × 90 cm = 270 cm or 2 m 70 cm **2)** 4 × 40 cm = 160 cm or 1 m 60 cm **3)** 5 × 30 cm = 150 cm or 1 m 50 cm **4)** 270 cm + 160 cm + 150 cm = 580 cm or 5 m 80 cm; 80 cm = $\frac{8}{10}$ of a metre **Task C: 1)** 1 m 80 cm; needs 2 planks **2)** Needs 10 planks; $\frac{2}{10}$ m will be left over from each plank **3)** 4 short pieces are 160 cm and 4 longer pieces are 200 cm; needs 1 plank for 2 shorts and 1 long so 2 planks would give 4 shorts and 2 long; a third plank can be used for the remaining 2 long pieces **4)** Children's own working

## In the classroom

Return to the image of the 'tenths' fraction bar. Re-establish that tenths are the result of dividing an object into ten equal parts. Children quickly recall the missing labels.

Now label the bar as '1 metre' and pose these, or similar, questions for different groups to consider:

- (Indicate the midway point.) *How can we describe this point as a fraction of a metre?* $\left(\frac{1}{2} \text{ or } \frac{5}{10}\right)$
- *What measurement does each tenth of the metre stick represent? How do you know?*
- *What fraction of a metre is 80 cm? Is it more or less than $\frac{3}{4}$ of a metre? How do you know?*

Establish that each tenth is 10 cm as there are 100 cm in a metre. Children should discuss the value of other fractions of the metre, e.g. $\frac{4}{10}$. Language such as: *'There are ten equal parts and I have four of them'* will support this.

A second metre bar can then be introduced to start to explore measurements that are more than 1 metre. These can be expressed as metres, e.g. $1\frac{3}{10}$ m, and then in metres and centimetres, e.g. 1 m 30 cm.

Pose these, or similar, questions for different groups to consider:

- *A shop sells planks $1\frac{3}{10}$ metres long. How much more than a metre is each plank? What is this in centimetres?*
- *I buy three planks. Will I have exactly 4 metres of wood? How do you know?*
- *How many planks will I need to buy so that I have at least 5 metres of wood?*

# Task A (Guided learning with an adult)

| | | | |
|---|---|---|---|
| $\frac{7}{10}$ m | 1 m 10 cm | $\frac{9}{10}$ m | ? |
| $\frac{4}{10}$ m | 60 cm | 10 cm | $\frac{2}{10}$ m |
| 80 cm | $\frac{10}{10}$ m | 50 cm | $\frac{3}{10}$ m |

There are 10 equal parts and I have _____ of them.

- Re-establish language using a metre strip, or a counting stick, as a model to show that there are ten equal parts and each is one tenth of a metre.
- Ask children to use each of the 12 measurements shown above to label the metre strip.
- Discuss what they will need to do to help with 1 m 10 cm. What is the problem here?
- The question mark can be used as a measurement of their choice.
- Ask children to use the labelled metre strip to independently explore objects in the classroom that are approximately $\frac{2}{10}$ of a metre.

# Task B (Independent task)

Help Jade decide how much wood she needs to build her garden bench. Give your answers in metres and centimetres.

1) Two long pieces for the seat and one for the back. Each piece is $\frac{9}{10}$ metre.
2) Four pieces for the legs. Each piece is $\frac{4}{10}$ metre.
3) Five pieces for the back. Each piece is $\frac{3}{10}$ metre.
4) How much does she need in total? _____ m _____ cm
   What fraction of a metre do the centimetres represent?

# Task C (Independent task)

Help Sid decide how many planks he should buy to start building a tree house. You can show your working as jumps on the number line.

The shop sells wood in $1\frac{3}{10}$ m planks.

1) Six steps for the ladder. Each step needs $\frac{3}{10}$ m of wood.
2) Ten pieces for the floor. Each piece needs to be 1 m 10 cm long.
   How much wood will he have left over from each piece?
   Give your answer in tenths.
3) Four short and four long pieces for the windows.
   The short pieces are 40 cm and the long pieces are $\frac{5}{10}$ metre.
   What is the least number of planks that Sid must buy?
4) Five pieces for the door. Each piece is _____ tenths of a metre.

You decide the length of the pieces for the door!

# UNIT 7  Compare and order fractions (with the same denominator)

## National Curriculum link:

Compare and order unit fractions, and fractions with the same denominators.

## Year 3 pupils should already know that:

- Fractions are numbers in their own right
- The denominator determines the number of equal parts the whole is divided into and the numerator shows how many of these equal parts are represented by the fraction
- Fractions with the same denominator are easier to compare

## Supporting understanding

In the same way it is easier to order measurements that are all in the same unit, e.g. all in millilitres, it is also much easier to compare and order a set of fractions that share the same denominator.

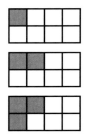

Images are useful to provide a pictorial representation and, later on, to help children compare fractions that do not share the same denominator.

This unit also uses simple equivalent fractions to help when ordering.

## Using simple equivalent fractions

In Key Stage 1, children will have met two quarters as the equivalent of one half. In previous units, there are many opportunities to identify halves when exploring non-unit fractions.

These include $\frac{2}{4}, \frac{3}{6}, \frac{4}{8}$ and $\frac{5}{10}$. Some groups may also have gone on to consider $\frac{6}{12}$ or even $\frac{10}{20}$.

Using equal-sized bars will help children to secure this understanding.

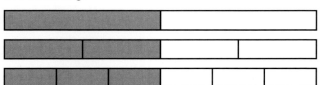

**ANSWERS**
**Task A:** $\frac{3}{10}, \frac{5}{10}, \frac{6}{10}, \frac{7}{10}$ and $\frac{2}{8}, \frac{3}{8}, \frac{4}{8}, \frac{5}{8}$ **Task B:** $\frac{1}{8}, \frac{2}{8}(\frac{1}{4}), \frac{3}{8}, \frac{4}{8}(\frac{1}{2}), \frac{5}{8}, \frac{7}{8}$
and $\frac{1}{6}, \frac{2}{6}, \frac{3}{6}(\frac{1}{2}), \frac{4}{6}, \frac{5}{6}$ **Task C: 1)** Zack: set of five eighths fractions in order, e.g. $\frac{1}{8}, \frac{3}{8}, \frac{4}{8}$, etc. **2)** Abi: set of three sixths fractions in order, e.g. $\frac{1}{6}, \frac{2}{6}, \frac{4}{6}$, etc. **3)** E.g. $\frac{1}{8}, \frac{2}{8}(\frac{1}{4}$ from Billy), $\frac{3}{8}, \frac{4}{8}(\frac{1}{2}$ from Billy), $\frac{5}{8}, \frac{6}{8}$
($\frac{3}{4}$ from Billy), $\frac{7}{8}, \frac{8}{8}$ **4)** E.g. $\frac{1}{6}, \frac{2}{6}(\frac{1}{3}$ from Billy), $\frac{3}{6}(\frac{1}{2}$ from Billy), $\frac{4}{6}$
($\frac{2}{3}$ from Billy), $\frac{5}{6}, \frac{6}{6}$ **Challenge:** Children's own ideas, e.g. tenths, where Billy has $\frac{1}{5}, \frac{1}{2}$ and $\frac{3}{5}$

## In the classroom

Revisit the key point that fractions are numbers in their own right, but it is important to know how they compare to each other and how we can order them.

Invite children to consider John's problem.

$\frac{7}{8}$      $\frac{1}{3}$      $\frac{5}{8}$      $\frac{3}{8}$

> Hmm, I need to order these fractions.

- *Why might John find this difficult?*
- *Which fraction do you think John would like to change to make this easier for him?*
- *Describe a different fraction that John might like.*

Agree that it is easier to order fractions when they all have the same denominator. Order John's fractions (eighths), including the new one suggested, using images and previous language structures: *'There are … equal parts and I have … of them. I have …'* to help make decisions.

Provide children with different groups of fractions to order, e.g. quarters, fifths and sixths.

Encourage them to use the language structure to help.

Consider the following group of fractions:

$\frac{7}{10}$      $\frac{1}{10}$      $\frac{3}{10}$      $\frac{1}{2}$      $\frac{9}{10}$

- *What do you notice this time?*
- *What facts could we use to help us sort this out?*

Establish that we can order fractions that do not have the same denominator and that using knowledge of equivalence (to $\frac{1}{2}$ in this case) will help us here, and may help in the work we are doing next.

## Task A (Independent task)

You will need fraction image cards. Shuffle the cards.

  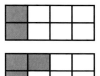 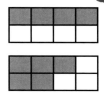

- Use the language: *'There are ____ equal parts and I have ____ of them. I have ____'* to name each fraction.
- Sort the fraction cards into groups that share the same denominator.
- Compare and order the fractions in each group.
- Write the fractions in each group in order.

## Task B (Independent task)

Provide children with the fraction image cards shown below. Shuffle the cards.

   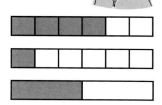

- Use the language: *'There are ____ equal parts and I have ____ of them. I have ____'* to name each fraction.
- Sort the fraction cards into groups that have the same denominator.
- Compare and order the fractions in each group.
- Which two fractions have you not used? How can you find a way to use them?

## Task C (Independent task or guided learning with an adult)

 I collect fraction cards with eighths.

**Zack**

 I collect fraction cards with sixths.

**Abi**

 I do not collect fraction cards with eighths or sixths, but I do collect other fractions!

**Billy**

- Zack has five different fraction cards.
- Abi has three different fraction cards.
- Billy has three different cards.

1) Make up a set of fractions for Zack and write them in order.
2) Make up a set of fractions for Abi and write them in order.

3) Now find three different fractions for Billy that can be used in Zack's set. Write the new set in order.
4) Now do the same for Abi's set.

**Challenge:**

Choose your own set of fractions. Find three different fractions that Billy can use with your set. Write them all in order.

# UNIT 8 — Compare and order unit fractions

## National Curriculum link:
**Compare and order unit fractions, and fractions with the same denominators.**

## Year 3 pupils should already know that:
- Unit fractions all have numerators with the value of 1
- The denominator determines the number of equal parts there are in the whole
- It is easier to compare and order fractions with the same denominator

## Supporting understanding

Providing a strong visual for fractions helps children to make comparisons and decisions about their value, and their position on the number line.

By using equal-sized bars, unit and non-unit fractions can be easily compared. Many fractions are more difficult to represent using the familiar pizza image.

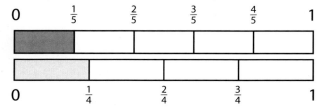

## Unit fractions on the number line

As in previous units, we are using equal-sized fraction bars labelled 0 to 1, so we can relate these images directly to the number line.

A powerful visual is to lay one fraction bar on top of the other so that the detail on each is still visible, or to place one above a number line and one below it.

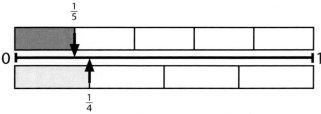

It is clear to see now that $\frac{1}{5}$ is smaller than $\frac{1}{4}$ and comes before it on the number line.

Bars can be extended to compare numbers such as $1\frac{1}{5}$ and $1\frac{1}{4}$ or $4\frac{1}{5}$ and $4\frac{1}{4}$ in the same way.

### ANSWERS
**Task A:** Pairs of unit fractions compared using the 'less than' sign; then in order $\frac{1}{6}$, $\frac{1}{5}$, $\frac{1}{4}$, $\frac{1}{3}$, $\frac{1}{2}$ **Task B:** Pairs of unit fractions compared using the 'less than' sign and then children's own number lines comparing two fractions at a time **Challenge:** Three fractions ordered on a number line **Task C:** Children's own number lines comparing two or three fractions at a time **3)** Use additional fraction bars to represent the one whole in each number and then just compare $\frac{1}{6}$ and $\frac{1}{5}$ **Challenge:** $\frac{1}{8}$, $\frac{1}{5}$ and $\frac{1}{3}$

## In the classroom

Revisit the key point that it is easier to compare fractions with the same denominator. However, we can use what we know about denominators to help us compare fractions with the same numerator, but different denominators, e.g. $\frac{1}{2}$ and $\frac{1}{4}$.

Invite children to discuss the following problem.
- Sally and Zack each have the same size of pizza.
- Sally says: 'Pete, you can have $\frac{1}{4}$ of my pizza.'
- Zack says: 'Pete, you can have $\frac{1}{5}$ of my pizza.'

  Pete loves pizza. Whose offer should he choose? Why?

Ask children to draw images to help prove their answer.

*Unfortunately, Pete made the wrong choice! Why do you think he did that? How would you explain to Pete the error he has made?*

Use the fraction bar image opposite to help secure children's understanding of comparing a quarter to a fifth.

Record as: $\frac{1}{5} < \frac{1}{4}$.

Relate the two images to a number line from 0 to 1. Place one image above the number line and the other below it.
*What do you notice? Which fraction comes first on the number line?*

Reinforce this concept by comparing another pair of unit fractions, e.g. $\frac{1}{3}$ and $\frac{1}{6}$.

Pose these, or similar, questions for different groups to consider before finally looking at the positions of the fractions on a number line:
- *How can you describe the fraction bar showing $\frac{1}{3}$?*
- *What do you notice about the fraction bars for thirds and sixths?*
- *How do these fractions compare to $\frac{1}{4}$?*

# Task A (Independent task)

You will need a set of cut-out fraction bars.
Shuffle the bars.

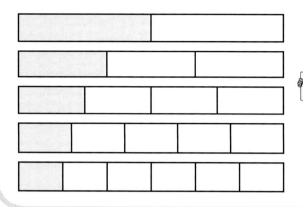

1) Label the fractions on each bar.

2) Choose pairs of unit fractions to compare.

3) Record what you have found using the 'less than' symbol, e.g.

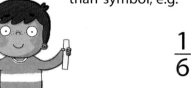

$$\frac{1}{6} < \frac{1}{3}$$

4) Now write all the unit fractions in order from smallest to largest.

# Task B (Independent task or guided learning with an adult)

Children will need a set of cut-out fraction bars as in Task A.

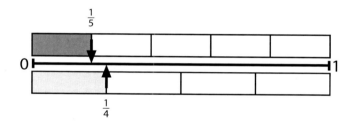

- Label each unit fraction and begin to make some comparisons, e.g. $\frac{1}{6} < \frac{1}{3}$.
- Children should draw number lines with a ruler.
- Use the fraction bars to help order pairs of fractions on the number line, e.g.

**Challenge:**
Find a way to show the order of three fractions on the number line.

# Task C (Independent task)

You will need a set of cut-out fraction bars as in Task A, but include the additional bars below.
Shuffle the bars.

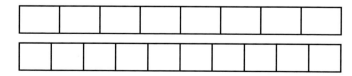

1) Label each unit fraction and begin to make some comparisons, e.g. $\frac{1}{6} < \frac{1}{3}$.

2) Use the fraction bars to help order two or three fractions on the number line.

    Show your number lines.

3) How could you compare $1\frac{1}{6}$ and $1\frac{1}{5}$?

**Challenge:**
Zack drew this number line. Which three fractions was he comparing?

# UNIT 9  Finding fractions of a set of objects

## National Curriculum link:

**Recognise, find and write fractions of a discrete set of objects: unit fractions and non-unit fractions with small denominators.**

## Year 3 pupils should already know that:

- Unit fractions all have numerators with the value of 1
- The denominator determines the number of equal parts there are in the whole
- We use division to find a fraction of an amount or set of objects

## Supporting understanding

Children will grasp this concept more easily if they have previously experienced the 'whole' as not necessarily being 'one'.

To find the fraction of an amount, or a set of objects, we must view the set as the 'whole', i.e. the whole set or whole amount.

Fraction bars and other images can be used to show how the 'whole' can be split into fractions.

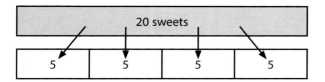

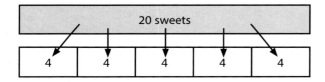

## Using multiplication and division facts

It is vital for children to recognise the relationship between fractions and division if they are to secure understanding.

Making links using language structures helps to reinforce this relationship.

> One **quarter** of **20** is **5** as **20** divided by **4** is **5**.

**ANSWERS**
**Task A:** Children use large fraction strips to explore finding a half, third or quarter of different whole sets
**Task B: 1)** 4  **2)** 5  **3)** E.g. $\frac{1}{4}$ of 12 and $\frac{1}{5}$ of 15  **4)** E.g. $\frac{1}{2}$ and $\frac{1}{3}$ (or even $\frac{1}{6}$)  **Task C:** E.g. roll a 3 and find $\frac{1}{3}$ of 18, 24, 30, etc.

## In the classroom

> Revisit the key point that the denominator shows the number of equal parts there are in the whole.
>
> Check that children are secure with this by asking about the number of parts the whole has been divided into for halves, thirds, quarters, fifths, etc.

> Explain that using knowledge of division can also help us when we are trying to find a fraction of a set of objects. The set of objects can be described as the whole.
>
> *Consider a set of 20 objects, for example sweets, or a measurement such as 20 metres. This is the whole. I want to find a quarter of the whole set.*
>
> *What should I do?*

> Ask children to discuss the problem and make suggestions.
>
> Establish that you can find a quarter by dividing by four.

> Use the visual representation of the whole (as shown opposite) and then model by dividing into four equal parts, e.g. sharing 20 between 4.
>
> Using a language structure, establish that: *'One quarter of 20 is 5 as 20 divided by 4 is 5.'*
>
> Point out that we can also find a quarter by halving a half.

> Focus on the use of multiplication and division facts to help identify fractions of a whole set.
>
> Pose these, or similar, questions for different groups to consider:

- *I know the 5 times table. What fractions will this help me with?*
- *What multiplication fact should I use to find $\frac{1}{5}$ of 20?*
- *I used the division fact 30 ÷ 5 = 6 to help me find a fraction of a whole set. What was I trying to find out?*

# Task **A** (Guided learning with an adult)

- Use paper to create a set of large fraction strips.
- Use cubes or counters to represent the whole set each time, e.g. 12, and then other fraction strips to explore finding fractions of amounts by sharing into equal groups.

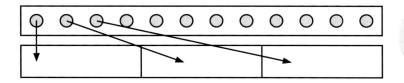

One **third** of **12** is **4** as **12** divided by **3** is **4**.

- Use the language structure to help describe each example.
- Explore finding a half, third or quarter of different whole sets.

# Task **B** (Independent task)

| 12 |
|----|

| 15 |
|----|

Use Cuisenaire rods or integer bars to help explore fractions of these wholes.

**1)** What is $\frac{1}{3}$ of 12?

**2)** What is $\frac{1}{3}$ of 15?

**3)** What other fractions of these wholes can you find?

**HINT:** Remember that 'thirds' means three equal parts. Which three rods can you use?

Record what you find out.

**4)** Now make other wholes with the rods, e.g. 18 with a 10 and 8 rod. What fractions of this whole can you find?

# Task **C** (Independent task)

| 18 | 35 | 16 |
|----|----|----|
| 32 | 24 | 30 |
| 40 | 36 | ?  |

- Roll a dice to make fractions, e.g.  makes a fifth. **Make a tenth if you roll a 1**.
- Think about the multiplication table that will help you with your fraction.
- Choose a number from the grid for your whole.
- Now find your fraction of this whole.
- Write down the division fact that helped you.

You may find this language useful:

One **fifth** of **20** is **4** as **20** divided by **5** is **4**.

# UNIT 10 Find and recognise fractions of a set

## National Curriculum link:

Recognise, find and write fractions of a discrete set of objects: unit fractions and non-unit fractions with small denominators.

## Year 3 pupils should already know that:

- Unit fractions all have numerators with the value of 1
- The denominator determines the number of equal parts there are in the whole
- We use division to find a fraction of an amount or set of objects

## Supporting understanding

In Unit 9, children began to explore unit fractions of a set. They made links to multiplication and division facts to help make decisions.

This language structure will continue to support understanding in this unit.

> One **quarter** of **20** is **5** as **20** divided by **4** is **5**.

## Recognising fractions of a set

Resources like Cuisenaire rods, integer bars or cubes are useful as a starting point here.

Imagine that we want to identify what fraction 3 is of 12. By representing the whole and the 3, children can explore how many of the three rods equal the whole.

| 12 | | | |
|---|---|---|---|

| 3 |
|---|

| 3 | 3 | 3 | 3 |
|---|---|---|---|

In doing so, we find that 3 represents $\frac{1}{4}$ of 12. We can also use the grouping model of division to confirm that $12 \div 3 = 4$ or there are 4 groups of 3 in 12.

## In the classroom

> Revisit the language: *One fifth of 20 is 4, as 20 divided by 5 is 4.*
>
> *How can we prove this is correct? What can we visualise or draw?*

> Introduce the problem that will be developed during the lesson.
>
> *The toy shop sells red, blue and green marbles in three different-sized jars.*
>
>
>
> *Billy and Abi want to buy some marbles. Billy decides to buy $\frac{1}{4}$ of a jar.*

> Pose these, or similar, questions for different groups to consider:
>
> - *How many blue marbles would Billy buy?*
> - *How many red marbles would Billy buy?*
> - *If Billy chooses green, how many more marbles would he have than if he chose red marbles?*

> Return to the language structure and the fraction bar images used in Unit 9 to confirm answers to the previous questions, e.g: *One quarter of 40 is 10, as 40 divided by 4 is 10.*

> *Abi only buys four marbles.*
>
> - *What do we need to find out?*
> - *What different fractions of each jar could this be?*

> Use a visual like Cuisenaire rods, integer bars or cubes to represent 24 as the whole. What fraction of 24 is 4? Ask children to discuss what we can do to help us.
>
> Model finding how many fours there are in 24 using rods (or similar).
>
> *We now have six equal parts and we know that a whole divided into six equal parts shows sixths. So 4 is $\frac{1}{6}$ of 24.*

**ANSWERS**
**Task A:** $\frac{1}{2}$ of 24 = 12, $\frac{1}{3}$ of 24 = 8 and $\frac{1}{4}$ of 24 = 6    **Task B: 1)** 48 ÷ 2 = 24, 48 ÷ 6 = 8, 48 ÷ 3 = 16, 48 ÷ 8 = 6 **2)** $\frac{1}{4}$ because there are four equal parts and these are quarters; there are 4 tens in 40
**Task C: 1)** Range of possible answers, e.g. buys 1 with 6 in whole jar ($\frac{1}{6}$ of 6 = 1), buys 2 with 12 in whole jar ($\frac{1}{6}$ of 12 = 2), etc.
**2)** 24 marbles ($\frac{1}{2}$ of 48), 16 marbles ($\frac{1}{3}$ of 48), 12 marbles ($\frac{1}{4}$ of 48), 8 marbles ($\frac{1}{6}$ of 48), etc.

# Task **A** (Guided learning with an adult)

Tom also wants to buy some red marbles, but he cannot work out what fraction to buy.

| 24 marbles |
|---|

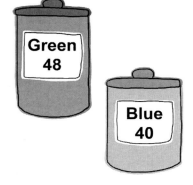

**Red**
**24**

**HINT:** You can use counters or cubes to help you.

Use what you know about sharing to find out how many marbles he could buy.
Write the fraction each time.

# Task **B** (Independent task)

**Green**
**48**

**Blue**
**40**

**1)** Help Pete and Jade to find out how many green marbles they will get if they buy the following fractions:

$\frac{1}{2}$   $\frac{1}{6}$   $\frac{1}{3}$   $\frac{1}{8}$

Write the division facts that helped you.

**2)** Pete then bought 10 blue marbles. What fraction of the whole jar is this?

Show how you worked this out.

# Task **C** (Independent task)

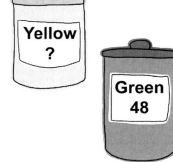

**Yellow**
**?**

**Green**
**48**

Sally and Fred also want to buy marbles. They have found a jar of yellow marbles on a shelf.

**1)** Sally buys $\frac{1}{6}$ of the yellow marble jar. Investigate how many marbles Sally buys and how many marbles were in the full jar.

How many different answers can you find?
Write your answers as $\frac{1}{6}$ of _____ = _____.

**2)** Fred buys an even number of green marbles. How many marbles could he buy? What fraction of 48 is this? Is there more than one solution?

# UNIT 11  Solving problems about fractions of amounts

## National Curriculum link:

**Recognise, find and write fractions of a discrete set of objects: unit fractions and non-unit fractions with small denominators.**

## Year 3 pupils should already know that:

* Unit fractions all have numerators with the value of 1
* The denominator determines the number of equal parts there are in the whole
* We use division to find a fraction of an amount or set of objects

## Supporting understanding

In previous units, images have been introduced to help children make sense of fractions and to work with them. This has included simply sharing into equal groups to find a fraction of an amount.

In this problem, children find different fractions of an amount and consider what is left, e.g.

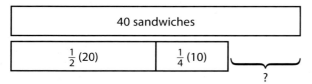

The fraction bar image can be adapted to help visualise the amount left, e.g. in this case 10 or $\frac{1}{4}$ of the whole.

## Solving problems

It is important that children have plenty of opportunities to apply knowledge and skills. This not only secures understanding, but also provides evidence of learning.

To be successful, children must first make sense of the problem and find a starting point. Encourage children to tell the story of the problem, role-play it or sketch something that helps them make sense of it.

As teachers, we need to model how to be a problem solver and show children how to find starting points.

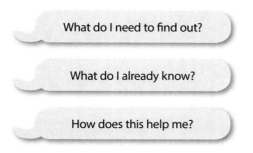

What do I need to find out?

What do I already know?

How does this help me?

**ANSWERS**
**Task A:** 16 fruit salads: $\frac{1}{2}$ is 8 and $\frac{1}{4}$ is 4; 12 soft drinks: $\frac{1}{2}$ is 6, $\frac{1}{4}$ is 3 and $\frac{1}{3}$ is 4 **Task B: 1)** 5 **2)** 6 **3)** $\frac{1}{6}$ **4)** 25 cups **5)** E.g. 10 biscuits is $\frac{1}{6}$ of 60 **Task C:** Table 2: 2 coffees, 2 teas, 6 biscuits and 2 sandwiches; Table 3: 3 coffees, 5 teas, 9 biscuits and 5 sandwiches
**Challenge:** $\frac{1}{20}$

## In the classroom

Introduce the problem that will be developed throughout the lesson:

*The local café is preparing for the next day. The team is deciding how many cakes and biscuits to bake and how many sandwiches to make.*

*They decide to bake 36 cakes and 60 biscuits and to make 40 sandwiches.*

*Bob bakes $\frac{1}{6}$ of the cakes, Oz bakes $\frac{1}{6}$ of the biscuits and Ellie makes $\frac{1}{2}$ of the sandwiches.*

Ask different groups to work on the fractions, $\frac{1}{2}$ of 40 being the least challenging.

* *What fraction of sandwiches does Ellie still need to make?*
* *What fractions of cakes and biscuits are still left to bake?*

*After 30 minutes, Bob has baked another $\frac{1}{4}$ of the cakes needed. Oz has baked another $\frac{1}{5}$ of the biscuits and Ellie has made another $\frac{1}{4}$ of the sandwiches.*

* *How many more of each item have they prepared?*
* *How many do they still have left to make?*

*Ellie makes another 8 sandwiches.*

* *What fraction is this of the total of 40 sandwiches? How do you know?*
* *How many sandwiches must she still make?*

Remodel as required and encourage children to use appropriate language to explain their thinking.

*Everything was made on time and the café is now open for business! Bob switches on the machine for hot water. It holds enough for 30 cups of tea or coffee.*

Ask children to work on different problems about the items sold in the café that day.

## Task A (Independent task)

The café also sells fruit salads and soft drinks.
They had 16 fruit salads to sell and
12 soft drinks.

Find these fractions of each.

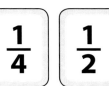
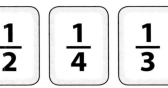

## Task B (Independent task)

The café has 36 cakes, 60 biscuits and 40 sandwiches to sell.
The hot water machine holds enough for 30 cups of tea or coffee.

1) Table 1 ordered $\frac{1}{8}$ of the sandwiches. How many sandwiches did they order?
2) They also ordered $\frac{1}{6}$ of the cakes. How many cakes did they order?
3) What fraction of the hot water was used for the drinks for Table 1?
4) How many more cups of tea or coffee can the café make before they have to refill the machine?
5) Choose the number of biscuits ordered and write this as a fraction of the total biscuits baked.

**Table 1**

2 coffees

3 teas

_____ cakes

_____ sandwiches

? biscuits

## Task C (Guided learning with an adult)

The café has 36 cakes, 60 biscuits and 40 sandwiches to sell.
The hot water machine holds enough for 30 cups of tea or coffee.

Use the clues to find out what each table ordered at the café.

- The total number of drinks ordered by Table 2 was a half of the number ordered by Table 3.
- Altogether, the two tables ordered $\frac{1}{4}$ of the total number of biscuits baked.
- Table 3 ordered $\frac{1}{8}$ of the total number of sandwiches made.
- The number of teas ordered by Table 2 was a third of the number of biscuits ordered.
- Only $\frac{1}{6}$ of the hot water in the machine was used for the tea on Table 3.

**Challenge:**
What fraction of the total number of sandwiches was ordered by Table 2?

**Table 2**

_____ coffees

2 teas

_____ biscuits

2 sandwiches

**Table 3**

3 coffees

_____ teas

_____ biscuits

_____ sandwiches

**UNIT 12**

# Adding fractions (tenths)

## National Curriculum link:

**Add** and subtract **fractions with the same denominator within one whole** [for example, $\frac{5}{7} + \frac{1}{7} = \frac{6}{7}$].

## Year 3 pupils should already know that:

- In a fraction, the denominator shows how many equal parts the whole has been divided into
- A whole can also be described as a fraction, e.g. fifths means there are five equal parts so the whole can be described as $\frac{5}{5}$
- It is much easier to add fractions when the denominators are the same

## Supporting understanding

In previous units, children have counted in different fraction steps, including tenths. Images have been used to support this understanding.

Children should be very familiar with fraction bars and other images. Remember that the counting stick is also a useful image as it provides an opportunity to look at a whole that is made up of tenths, i.e. $\frac{10}{10}$.

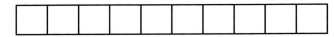

We can count along the stick in tenths and then begin to establish some addition calculations, e.g. start at $\frac{4}{10}$ and count on 3 more tenths.

This can then be written as $\frac{4}{10} + \frac{3}{10} = \frac{7}{10}$.

## Pairs of fractions that total a whole

It is vital that children have a secure understanding that a 'whole' can also be represented as a fraction. What it looks like will depend on the number of equal pieces it has been divided into, e.g. when the denominator is 8, then one whole can be represented as $\frac{8}{8}$.

We can also use our number bonds, along with visual representations, to explore pairs of fractions that total one whole.

Knowing that $3 + 5 = 8$ helps us to recognise that $\frac{3}{8} + \frac{5}{8} = \frac{8}{8}$, which we know is one whole.

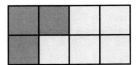

## In the classroom

Revisit the key point that the denominator in a fraction shows how many equal parts the whole has been divided into. Several different images showing e.g. fifths, quarters, eighths and tenths would be useful here.

Use the language: *'I know this whole is in … because I can count … equal parts.'*

Using a visual, such as the counting stick, practise counting on and back in tenths. Stop at different points and ask questions, such as:

- *How many more tenths must we count to complete the whole?* (Link this to the use of number bonds to 10.)
- *How many more tenths must we count to complete two wholes?* (Link this to the use of number bonds to 20.)

Continue by asking questions that require counting fractions within the whole, e.g.

- *I started on $\frac{2}{10}$ and landed on $\frac{7}{10}$. How many tenths have I counted?*
- *I counted on $\frac{4}{10}$ and landed on $\frac{9}{10}$. Where did I start?*
- *I am on $\frac{3}{10}$ and want to count on $\frac{1}{4}$. Why might I find this more difficult?*

Establish that it is much easier to count in or add fractions when the denominators are the same.

Relate the counting you have been doing with the addition of fractions, e.g. record it as $\frac{7}{10} + \frac{3}{10} = \frac{10}{10}$, $\frac{2}{10} + \frac{5}{10} = \frac{7}{10}$, etc.

**ANSWERS**
**Task A:** E.g. $\frac{1}{10} + \frac{9}{10} = \frac{10}{10}$, $\frac{2}{10} + \frac{8}{10} = \frac{10}{10}$, etc. **Task B:** E.g. $\frac{4}{10} + \frac{6}{10} = \frac{10}{10}$ and then $\frac{4}{10} + \frac{4}{10} = \frac{8}{10}$ **Task C:** E.g. $\frac{4}{10} + \frac{3}{10} = \frac{7}{10}$, $\frac{6}{10} + \frac{5}{10} = 1\frac{1}{10}$, etc. and then $\frac{1}{8} + \frac{3}{8} = \frac{4}{8}$, $\frac{6}{8} + \frac{4}{8} = 1\frac{2}{8}\left(1\frac{1}{4}\right)$, etc.

# Task **A** (Guided learning with an adult)

Start by using an image showing tenths. Agree that there are ten equal parts in the whole.

- Cover one of the parts. How many out of the ten parts are covered? Agree that this is 1 out of 10 and establish that this can be written as $\frac{1}{10}$.
- Now look at the number of parts that are not covered.
- Record the number sentence $\frac{1}{10} + \frac{9}{10} = \frac{10}{10}$ to represent this image. Link this to the number bonds of 10.
- Consider $\frac{2}{10}$ covered in the same way, using the language to describe the fraction.
- Work to explore other tenths.
- Remember to think about the number bonds of 10 and to record fraction number sentences.

> There are **10** equal parts and I have **1** of them. I have $\frac{1}{10}$.

# Task **B** (Independent task)

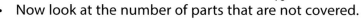

- Roll a dice to make a tenths fraction, e.g. $\frac{4}{10}$ if the dice shows 4.
- How many more tenths are needed to equal one whole?
- Write the addition calculation you used.
- How many more tenths are needed to equal $\frac{8}{10}$?
- Write the addition calculation you used this time.

# Task **C** (Independent task)

- Roll two dice to make two tenths fractions, e.g. $\frac{4}{10}$  and $\frac{3}{10}$ .
- Add the two fractions and write the calculation you used.
- How many different calculations can you make?

Now use the dice to make two new eighths fractions.

**HINT:** You may need to use mixed numbers to help you.

- How many different calculations can you make this time?

# UNIT 13  Solving problems about adding fractions

## National Curriculum link:

**Add** and subtract **fractions with the same denominator within one whole [for example, $\frac{5}{7} + \frac{1}{7} = \frac{6}{7}$].**

## Year 3 pupils should already know that:

- In a fraction the denominator shows how many equal parts the whole has been divided into
- A whole can also be described as a fraction, e.g. fifths means there are five equal parts so the whole can be described as $\frac{5}{5}$
- It is much easier to add fractions when the denominators are the same

## Supporting understanding

In Unit 12, children explored adding tenths up to 1. This unit extends to fractions with other denominators.

Fraction bars can be used to support counting on. It also supports the transition to using number lines, e.g. $\frac{3}{7} + \frac{2}{7}$:

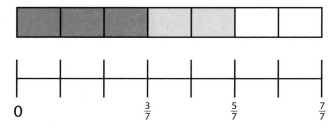

$$0 \qquad \frac{3}{7} \qquad \frac{5}{7} \qquad \frac{7}{7}$$

The number line can be extended to work with fractions beyond 1.

## Recording addition calculations on the number line

We can show calculations with fractions on a number line in the same way that we do with whole numbers.

Consider the addition $\frac{3}{8} + \frac{2}{8}$:

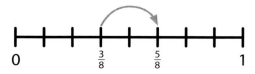

$$0 \qquad \frac{3}{8} \qquad \frac{5}{8} \qquad 1$$

The number line will later support calculations that bridge the whole, e.g. $\frac{5}{8} + \frac{4}{8}$ by partitioning $\frac{4}{8}$ into $\frac{3}{8}$ (to complete the whole) and $\frac{1}{8}$.

More able learners will be introduced to this as part of this unit.

## In the classroom

Show several different images, e.g. fifths, quarters, eighths and tenths would be useful here.

Invite children to choose one of the images (or visualise one of their own) and practise counting in these fraction steps up to one whole and then up to two wholes. More able children should be challenged to continue counting further in their fraction steps.

Pose these, or similar, questions for different groups to consider:

- *After you have counted your second fraction step, how many more steps must you take to complete the whole? How can you show this as a fraction? How might number bonds help you here?*

- *I want to count on two sixths. Why might I find it difficult to do this with the fractions you are counting in?*

Re-establish the key point that it is much easier to count in, or add, fractions when the denominators are the same.

Use one of the children's counts, e.g. $\frac{2}{5}$, and count on $\frac{3}{5}$ to complete the whole. Rewrite this as an addition calculation: $\frac{2}{5} + \frac{3}{5} = \frac{5}{5}$ or 1.

Model this on a fraction bar and then as jumps on the number line.

Reinforce this by asking children to quickly return to their own fraction count and practise writing fraction additions for some of the counting they have done, e.g. I start on $\frac{2}{8}$ and count on $\frac{3}{8}$ as $\frac{2}{8} + \frac{3}{8} = \frac{5}{8}$.

Encourage children to show their additions on a number line.

**ANSWERS**

**Task A: 1–3)** 1 or $\frac{8}{8}$ **4)** $\frac{5}{8}$ **5)** $\frac{6}{8}$ **6)** $\frac{4}{8}$ **7)** E.g. $\frac{2}{8} + \frac{1}{8} = \frac{3}{8}$

**Task B:** On number lines: **1)** $\frac{3}{8}$ **2)** $\frac{3}{8}$ **3)** $\frac{5}{7}$ **4)** $\frac{6}{7}$ **5)** $\frac{5}{6}$ **6)** $\frac{3}{6}$

**7)** $\frac{3}{8} + \frac{2}{8} = \frac{5}{8}$ **8)** $\frac{2}{7} + \frac{4}{7} = \frac{6}{7}$ **Task C:** On number lines: **1)** $\frac{2}{8}$

**2)** $1\frac{1}{8}$ **3)** $\frac{6}{7}$ **4)** $\frac{3}{9}$ **5)** $1\frac{5}{6}$ **6)** $\frac{4}{5}$ **7)** $\frac{3}{7} + \frac{6}{7} = 1\frac{2}{7}$ **8)** It could be, e.g. $\frac{5}{7} + \frac{3}{7} = 1\frac{1}{7}$; it could not be, e.g. $\frac{5}{8} + \frac{3}{8}$ as this equals 1

## Task **A** (Independent task)

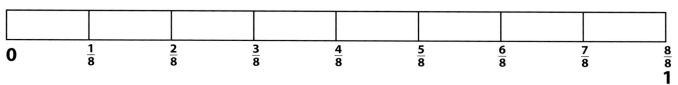

Copy and complete the calculations:

**1)** $\frac{7}{8} + \frac{1}{8} =$ _____

**2)** $\frac{6}{8} + \frac{2}{8} =$ _____

**3)** $\frac{5}{8} + \frac{3}{8} =$ _____

**4)** $\frac{4}{8} + \frac{1}{8} =$ _____

**5)** $\frac{5}{8} + \frac{1}{8} =$ _____

**6)** $\frac{3}{8} + \frac{1}{8} =$ _____

**7)** Now make up some more addition calculations of your own.

## Task **B** (Independent task)

Show the following calculations on a number line:

**1)** $\frac{2}{8} + \frac{1}{8} =$ _____

**2)** $\frac{5}{8} +$ _____ $= 1$

**3)** $\frac{3}{7} + \frac{2}{7} =$ _____

**4)** _____ $+ \frac{1}{7} = 1$

**5)** $\frac{3}{6} + \frac{2}{6} =$ _____

**6)** $\frac{2}{6} +$ _____ $= \frac{5}{6}$

What calculations do these number lines show?

**7)**

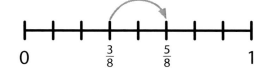

**8)**

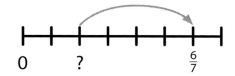

## Task **C** (Independent task or guided learning with an adult)

Show the following calculations on a number line:

**1)** $\frac{5}{8} + \frac{1}{8} +$ _____ $= 1$

**2)** $\frac{5}{8} + \frac{4}{8} =$ _____

**3)** _____ $+ \frac{2}{7} = 1\frac{1}{7}$

**4)** $\frac{8}{9} +$ _____ $= 1\frac{2}{9}$

**5)** $\frac{6}{6} + \frac{5}{6} =$ _____

**6)** _____ $+ \frac{3}{5} = 1\frac{2}{5}$

**7)** What calculation does the number line show?

E.g. _____ $+$ _____ $= 1\frac{2}{7}$

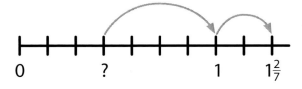

**8)** Tom drew a number line for his calculation:

$\frac{5}{?} + \frac{3}{?}$.

Tom's answer is greater than 1.

- What could his calculation be?
- What could it not be? Why?

# Subtracting fractions (1)

**UNIT 14**

## National Curriculum link:
Add and **subtract fractions with the same denominator within one whole** [for example, $\frac{5}{7} + \frac{1}{7} = \frac{6}{7}$].

## Year 3 pupils should already know that:
- In a fraction, the denominator shows how many equal parts the whole has been divided into
- A whole can also be described as a fraction, e.g. tenths means there are ten equal parts so the whole can be described as $\frac{10}{10}$
- It is much easier to subtract fractions when the denominators are the same

## Supporting understanding
In previous units, children have been counting on and back in fraction steps. This can be directly related to the number line using the fraction bar as a transitional image.

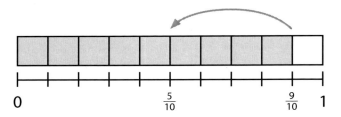

## Subtraction on the number line
We can show subtraction calculations with fractions on a number line in the same way that we do with whole numbers.

Consider the subtraction $\frac{7}{8} - \frac{3}{8}$:

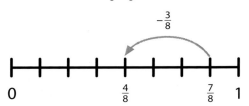

The number line will later support calculations that bridge the whole, e.g. $1\frac{2}{8} - \frac{3}{8}$ by partitioning $\frac{3}{8}$ into $\frac{2}{8}$ (to reach the whole) and $\frac{1}{8}$.

More able learners will be introduced to this as part of this unit.

## In the classroom

Using a visual, like a counting stick, practise counting on and back in tenths.
Stop at different points and ask questions, such as:

*How many more tenths must we count back to return to zero?*

Change the starting number to 1 or 2, etc. so children also count beyond 1:

*How many more tenths must we count back to return to 1?*

Link this to whole numbers.

Continue by asking questions that require counting fractions within the whole:

- *I start on $\frac{5}{10}$ and count back $\frac{2}{10}$. Where do I land?*
- *I started on $\frac{9}{10}$ and landed on $\frac{5}{10}$. How many tenths have I counted?*
- *I counted back $\frac{4}{10}$ and landed on $\frac{2}{10}$. Where did I start?*
- *I am on $\frac{7}{10}$ and want to count back $\frac{1}{4}$. Why might I find this more difficult?*

Establish that, as for addition, it is much easier to count back in or subtract fractions when the denominators are the same.

Relate the counting you have been doing with the subtraction of fractions, e.g. record it as $\frac{5}{10} - \frac{2}{10} = \frac{3}{10}$, $\frac{9}{10} - \frac{4}{10} = \frac{5}{10}$, etc.

Use one of the subtractions, e.g. $\frac{9}{10} - \frac{4}{10}$, and model it on the fraction bar. Use this to make links to the same calculation on the number line.

Now show a fraction bar and number line for eighths. This can be used in the same way.
Ask children to quickly practise $\frac{3}{8} - \frac{1}{8}$, $\frac{7}{8} - \frac{3}{8}$ and $\frac{7}{8} - \frac{6}{8}$.

**ANSWERS**
**Task A: 1)** $\frac{4}{8}$ **2)** $\frac{5}{8}$ **3)** $\frac{6}{8}$ **4)** $\frac{3}{8}$ **5)** $\frac{3}{8}$ **6)** $\frac{1}{8}$ **7)** E.g. $\frac{7}{8} - \frac{2}{8} = \frac{5}{8}$

**Task B:** On number lines: **1)** $\frac{3}{8}$ **2)** $\frac{5}{8}$ **3)** $\frac{4}{7}$ **4)** $\frac{5}{7}$ **5)** 0 **6)** $\frac{4}{6}$

**7)** $\frac{6}{7} - \frac{3}{7} = \frac{3}{7}$ **8)** $\frac{5}{8} - \frac{2}{8} = \frac{3}{8}$

**Task C:** On number lines: **1)** $\frac{3}{8}$ **2)** $\frac{3}{9}$ **3)** $\frac{3}{8}$ **4)** $\frac{2}{10}$ **5)** $\frac{9}{10}$ **6)** $1\frac{1}{8}$

**7)** $1\frac{2}{6} - \frac{5}{6} = \frac{3}{6}$ **8)** E.g. $1\frac{1}{10} - \frac{5}{10} = \frac{6}{10}$ or $1\frac{2}{9} - \frac{5}{9} = \frac{6}{9}$ or $1\frac{3}{8} - \frac{5}{8} = \frac{6}{8}$, etc.

## Task **A** (Independent task)

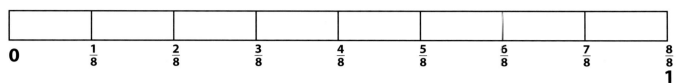

| 0 | $\frac{1}{8}$ | $\frac{2}{8}$ | $\frac{3}{8}$ | $\frac{4}{8}$ | $\frac{5}{8}$ | $\frac{6}{8}$ | $\frac{7}{8}$ | $\frac{8}{8}$ **1** |

Copy and complete the calculations:

**1)** $\frac{5}{8} - \frac{1}{8} = $ _____

**2)** $\frac{6}{8} - \frac{1}{8} = $ _____

**3)** $\frac{7}{8} - \frac{1}{8} = $ _____

**4)** $\frac{4}{8} - \frac{2}{8} = $ _____

**5)** $\frac{5}{8} - \frac{2}{8} = $ _____

**6)** $\frac{3}{8} - \frac{2}{8} = $ _____

**7)** Now make up some more subtraction calculations of your own.

## Task **B** (Independent task)

Show the following calculations on a number line:

**1)** $\frac{6}{8} - \frac{3}{8} = $ _____

**2)** $\frac{5}{8} - $ _____ $= 0$

**3)** $\frac{6}{7} - \frac{2}{7} = $ _____

**4)** _____ $- \frac{3}{7} = \frac{2}{7}$

**5)** $\frac{6}{6} - \frac{6}{6} = $ _____

**6)** $\frac{5}{6} - $ _____ $= \frac{1}{6}$

What calculations do these number lines show?

**7)**

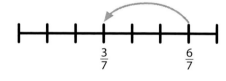

**8)**

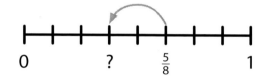

## Task **C** (Independent task)

Show the following calculations on a number line:

**1)** $\frac{8}{8} - \frac{1}{8} - $ _____ $= \frac{4}{8}$

**2)** $\frac{7}{9} - \frac{4}{9} = $ _____

**3)** $\frac{7}{8} - \frac{1}{2} = $ _____

**4)** $\frac{7}{10} - \frac{1}{2} = $ _____

**5)** $1\frac{2}{10} - \frac{3}{10} = $ _____

**6)** _____ $- \frac{3}{8} = \frac{6}{8}$

**7)** What calculation does this number line show?

E.g. $1\frac{2}{6} - $ _____ $= $ _____

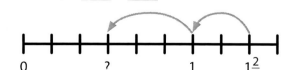

**8)** Jade subtracted this fraction: $\frac{5}{?}$ on her number line. Her answer was $\frac{6}{?}$.

- What could her calculation be? Think about what number **?** could be.
- Try to find more than one answer.

**UNIT 15  Finding the difference**

## National Curriculum link:

**Add and subtract fractions with the same denominator within one whole [for example, $\frac{5}{7} + \frac{1}{7} = \frac{6}{7}$].**

## Year 3 pupils should already know that:

- In a fraction, the denominator shows how many equal parts the whole has been divided into
- It is much easier to subtract fractions when the denominators are the same
- Finding the difference is another model of subtraction

## Supporting understanding

Children should know that they can also find the difference between two numbers to answer a subtraction calculation. The same is true of fractions.

Take the calculation $\frac{9}{10} - \frac{4}{10}$.

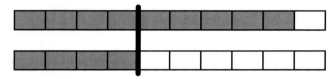

Up to the vertical line, both fractions are the same.

The difference can easily be seen and can be described in a variety of ways, e.g. $\frac{9}{10}$ is $\frac{5}{10}$ more than $\frac{4}{10}$, the difference between $\frac{9}{10}$ and $\frac{4}{10}$ is $\frac{5}{10}$, or $\frac{4}{10}$ is $\frac{5}{10}$ less than $\frac{9}{10}$.

## Using a number line

The same calculation can be shown on the number line. A transitional image is useful.

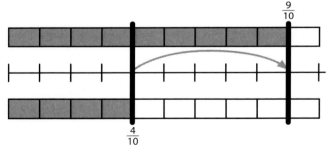

The number line between the two vertical lines shows clearly the relative position of the two fractions and how we can count on from $\frac{4}{10}$ to $\frac{9}{10}$ to find the difference.

By removing the fraction bar images, children should be able to see how the number line represents the same calculation.

## In the classroom

Use a simple calculation, e.g. 9 – 4, to revisit the key point that 'finding the difference' is another model of subtraction.

Use models and the language of 'same' and 'different' to secure understanding, e.g. 'same' is that both numbers have 4, 'different' is that 9 has 5 more.

Introduce the calculation $\frac{9}{10} - \frac{4}{10}$ and fraction bars to represent each fraction.

Ask children to describe what is the 'same' and what is 'different':

*In how many different ways can we describe the difference?*
(E.g. $\frac{9}{10}$ is $\frac{5}{10}$ more than $\frac{4}{10}$, etc.)

Use different sets of fraction bars for groups to compare in the same way, e.g. $\frac{4}{10}$ and $\frac{3}{10}$, $\frac{5}{8}$ and $\frac{3}{8}$, etc. (Provide fraction bar resources for some groups, as needed.)

Encourage children to describe the 'difference' and to create the subtraction calculation for each.

Model how the fraction bars can be used to help us make sense of these calculations on the number line.

Return to $\frac{9}{10} - \frac{4}{10}$.

As appropriate, groups should return to the fraction bars they have been comparing and link this to the calculation on the number line in the same way.

**ANSWERS**

**Task A:** As in example given  **Task B:** E.g. number line to show the difference between $\frac{9}{10}$ and $\frac{3}{10}$ with calculation $\frac{9}{10} - \frac{3}{10} = \frac{6}{10}$

**Challenge:** E.g. $\frac{8}{8}$ and $\frac{5}{8}$, $\frac{7}{8}$ and $\frac{4}{8}$, $\frac{6}{8}$ and $\frac{3}{8}$, etc.

**Task C:** Example solutions:

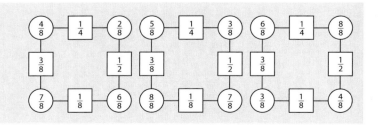

## Task **A** (Independent task)

You will need a set of fraction bars from $\frac{1}{10}$ to $\frac{10}{10}$.

1) Place all fraction bars face down on the table.
2) Pick two bars and write down the fractions.
3) Compare them and write down what is the 'same'.
4) Now write what is 'different'.
5) Put the bars back on the table and pick another two.

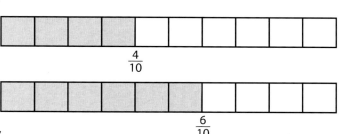

$\frac{4}{10}$

$\frac{6}{10}$

Example: $\frac{4}{10}$ and $\frac{6}{10}$

Same: $\frac{4}{10}$

Different: $\frac{6}{10}$ has $\frac{2}{10}$ more than $\frac{4}{10}$

## Task **B** (Independent task or guided learning with an adult)

You will need sets of tenths and eighths fraction bars.
Place the tenths bars face down on the table:

1) Pick pairs of bars each time.
2) Describe what is the 'same' and what is 'different' between the two fractions.
3) Show the difference using a number line.
4) Write the subtraction calculation that you used.

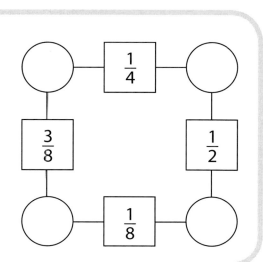

**Challenge:**

Ishmal chose a pair of fraction bars. The difference between them was $\frac{3}{8}$.
What fraction bars did he pick? Find more than one solution.

## Task **C** (Independent task or guided learning with an adult)

The fraction in each square is the 'difference' between the two circles on each side of it.

1) Use what you know and any resources to help find a solution.
2) Prove that your solution is correct by showing each difference on a number line.
3) Investigate to find if there is more than one solution to the problem.

$\frac{1}{4}$

$\frac{3}{8}$

$\frac{1}{2}$

$\frac{1}{8}$

# UNIT 16  Subtracting fractions (2)

## National Curriculum link:

Add and **subtract fractions with the same denominator within one whole** [for example, $\frac{5}{7} + \frac{1}{7} = \frac{6}{7}$].

## Year 3 pupils should already know that:

- In a fraction, the denominator shows how many equal parts the whole has been divided into.
- A whole can also be described as a fraction, e.g. tenths means there are ten equal parts so the whole can be described as $\frac{10}{10}$
- It is much easier to add and subtract fractions when the denominators are the same

## Supporting understanding

In previous units, children have added and subtracted pairs of fractions with the same denominator using images, including the number line, to help them.

In each case, the calculation to be carried out was generally explicit. In this unit, children will also need to decide on the operation to use.

Resources, such as fraction bars and other images, should be made available.

In this problem, the images used show containers.

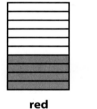
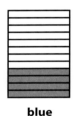

**red**          **yellow**          **blue**

## Developing problem solvers

It is important that children have plenty of opportunities to apply knowledge and skills.

This not only secures understanding but also provides evidence of learning.

To be successful, children must first make sense of the problem and find a starting point.

They must also decide how best to organise what they do and what they find out.

As teachers, we need to model how to be a problem solver and show children how to organise their thinking.

## In the classroom

Introduce the problem that will be developed throughout the lesson:

*At Sports Day, Class 3 are taking part in the water race.*

*There are three teams: red, yellow and blue.*

*The containers [to the left] show the water collected so far.*

---

Ask different groups to work on the different containers, blue being the most challenging.

*What fraction of the container has been collected so far?*

*What fraction still needs to be collected to fill the container?*

---

*Two children from each team have run so far.*

*What different fractions could each child have collected? Prove how you know.*

---

Model the use of lists to help children organise their findings and to check that all possibilities have been found.

Discuss what calculations they have used.

Ask children to quickly record the addition sentences.

---

*The next runner in the red team collected another $\frac{2}{10}$.*

*The next runners in the other teams collected enough water so that only $\frac{3}{?}$ of the container is left.*

*How much is in each container now?*

*What calculation did you use to help you?*

---

*The next teams (green, orange and purple) are ready for the water race.*

Ask different groups to work on the problems for the different teams and to record the calculations they use to help them.

**ANSWERS**

**Task A: 1)** E.g. $\frac{4}{10}$ and $\frac{1}{10}$, $\frac{3}{10}$ and $\frac{2}{10}$, etc. **2)** $\frac{3}{10}$ **3)** $\frac{7}{10}$ **4)** $\frac{3}{10}$

**Task B: 1)** E.g. Sami $\frac{1}{8}$, Ishmal $\frac{2}{8}$, Abi $\frac{3}{8}$; $\frac{2}{8}$, $\frac{2}{8}$; etc. **2)** $\frac{3}{8}$ **3)** $\frac{5}{8}$ **4)** $\frac{3}{8}$

**Task C: 1)** Jen $\frac{6}{12}$ and Li $\frac{1}{12}$, Jen $\frac{5}{12}$ and Li $\frac{2}{12}$ **2)** $\frac{4}{12}$ **3)** E.g. $\frac{3}{12}$, $\frac{4}{12}$ and $\frac{2}{12}$ (totalling $\frac{9}{12}$) **4)** $\frac{3}{12}$ each or $\frac{1}{4}$

## Task **A** (Guided learning with an adult)

**1)** Pete and Jade collected the water shown here:
What fraction of the container could they each have collected?
How many different possibilities can you find?

**2)** The next runner bumps into the container and $\frac{2}{10}$ of the water spills out!
What fraction is left now?

**3)** The last runner collects another $\frac{4}{10}$ of water.
What fraction do they have now?

**4)** What fraction do they still need to fill the container?

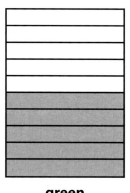

**green**

## Task **B** (Independent task)

**1)** Sami, Ishmal and Abi collected the water shown here.
What fraction of the container could they each have collected?
How many different possibilities can you find?

**2)** The next runner bumps into the container and $\frac{3}{8}$ of the water spills out!
What fraction is left now?

**3)** The last runner collects another $\frac{1}{4}$.
What fraction do they have now?

**4)** What fraction do they still need to fill the container?

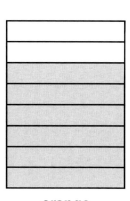

**orange**

## Task **C** (Independent task)

**1)** Jen and Li collected the water shown here. Jen collected at least $\frac{2}{12}$ more than Li.
What fraction of the container could they each have collected?
How many different possibilities can you find?

**2)** The next runner bumps into the container and some water spills out!
The water left fills exactly $\frac{1}{4}$ of the container.
What fraction was spilt?

**3)** The last three runners fill the container.
What fraction could they each have collected?
How many different possibilities can you find?

**4)** Each of the runners could have collected the same fraction of water.
What fraction is this? Can it be written in another way?

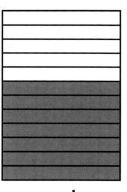

**purple**

# UNIT 17  Equivalent fractions

## National Curriculum link:

**Recognise and show, using diagrams, equivalent fractions with small denominators.**

## Year 3 pupils should already know that:

- Fractions can be represented by a range of images
- All fractions can be placed on the number line and some will sit in the same place as others
- Some fractions have the same value but may not look the same, e.g. $\frac{1}{2}$ and $\frac{2}{4}$

## Supporting understanding

In Key Stage 1, children will already have met the equivalent fractions $\frac{1}{2}$ and $\frac{2}{4}$ through a range of images.

Circular fraction images will also have supported understanding of a half hour or a quarter of an hour, and that $\frac{1}{2}$ hour = $\frac{2}{4}$ hour.

Language structures can also be used to secure the concept of equivalence.

> I know these fractions are equivalent because they have the same value.

> $\frac{2}{4}$ is equivalent to $\frac{1}{2}$ because they are both worth the same fraction of a whole.

## Introducing equivalence

Using two fraction bars the same length provides a useful image showing which fractions are equivalent.

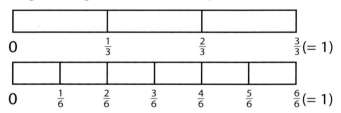

The image clearly shows that $\frac{1}{3} = \frac{2}{6}$ and $\frac{2}{3} = \frac{4}{6}$. Therefore, on the number line, these pairs of fractions will also have the same position.

This means that the numbers $1\frac{1}{3}$ and $1\frac{2}{6}$, $2\frac{1}{3}$ and $2\frac{2}{6}$, etc. will also have the same positions.

### ANSWERS
**Task A:** $\frac{1}{2} = \frac{2}{4}$, $\frac{1}{2} = \frac{3}{6}$, $\frac{1}{2} = \frac{4}{8}$ and $\frac{1}{2} = \frac{5}{10}$; twice

**Task B: 1)** $\frac{1}{3} = \frac{2}{6}$, $\frac{1}{3} = \frac{3}{9}$  **2)** The numerator goes into the denominator 3 times, it is $\frac{1}{3}$ of the denominator; the denominator is 3 times larger than the numerator  **3)** $\frac{4}{12}$, $\frac{5}{15}$, etc.

**Task C: 1)** $\frac{4}{20}$ not $\frac{5}{20}$, $\frac{6}{30}$ not $\frac{5}{30}$  **2)** The numerator goes into the denominator 5 times, it is $\frac{1}{5}$ of the denominator; the denominator is 5 times larger than the numerator  **3)** $\frac{7}{35}$, $\frac{8}{40}$, etc.

**4)** $\frac{5}{20} = \frac{1}{4}$ and $\frac{5}{30} = \frac{1}{6}$  **5)** We can use the same facts, e.g. $1\frac{2}{10}$

## In the classroom

> Revisit the key point that some fractions have the same value but may not look the same.

> Use the circular images (left) or similar. Ask children to explain what is the same and what is different about the two images.

> Use this language: $\frac{2}{4}$ is equivalent to $\frac{1}{2}$ because they are both worth the same fraction of a whole.

> Use a range of images (including fraction bars) where $\frac{1}{2}$, $\frac{1}{4}$ and $\frac{1}{3}$ are shown in different ways, e.g:

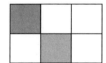 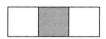

> Ask different groups to search for sets of equivalent fractions ($\frac{1}{2}$ being least challenging and $\frac{1}{3}$ most challenging) and practise using the language structure.

> Return to the fraction $\frac{1}{4}$ and agree the other fraction images that have the same value, i.e. $\frac{2}{8}$, $\frac{3}{12}$. Pose these, or similar, questions for different groups to consider:

- *What do you notice about the relationship between the numerator and denominator? How many 2s are in 8? How many 3s are in 12?*

- *What do you think comes next in this sequence of equivalent fractions? Why?*

> Establish the importance of multiplication and division facts. Each numerator is $\frac{1}{4}$ of the denominator and each denominator is 4 times larger than the numerator.

> We will use this information and the fraction bars to help us search for other sets of equivalent fractions.

## Task **A** (Guided learning with an adult)

You will need a set of fraction bars.

- Find the fraction bar that shows halves.
- Find other fractions that are worth the same as $\frac{1}{2}$.
- Write them down as $\frac{1}{2} =$ _____ .
- Practise using this language each time:
- How many times does the number on the top of the fraction go into the number on the bottom?

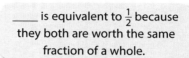

_____ is equivalent to $\frac{1}{2}$ because they both are worth the same fraction of a whole.

## Task **B** (Independent task)

**1)** You will need a set of fraction bars.
- Find the fraction bar that shows thirds.
- Find other fractions that are worth the same as $\frac{1}{3}$.
- Write them down as $\frac{1}{3} =$ _____ .
- Practise using this language each time:

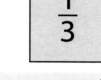

_____ is equivalent to $\frac{1}{3}$ because they both are worth the same fraction of a whole.

**2)** How can you describe the relationship between the numerator and denominator each time? Remember to think about multiplication facts.

**3)** What other fractions are equivalent to $\frac{1}{3}$? You will not have fraction bars for these.

## Task **C** (Independent task)

Abi used the relationship between the numerator and denominator to help her find fractions that are equivalent to $\frac{1}{5}$.

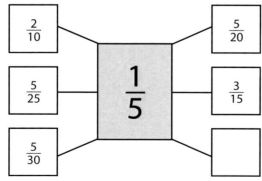

_____ is equivalent to $\frac{1}{5}$ because they both are worth the same fraction of a whole.

**1)** Check Abi's work and correct any mistakes she has made.

**2)** What is the relationship between the numerator and denominator for equivalent fractions of $\frac{1}{5}$?

**3)** Find some more equivalent fractions for the blank box.

**4)** Are the incorrect fractions equivalent to other fractions you know?

**5)** How might knowing equivalents for $\frac{1}{5}$ help you to find equivalents for $1\frac{1}{5}$?

# UNIT 18  More equivalent fractions

## National Curriculum link:
Recognise and show, using diagrams, equivalent fractions with small denominators.

## Year 3 pupils should already know that:
- Fractions can be represented by a range of images
- All fractions can be placed on the number line and some will sit in the same place as others
- Some fractions have the same value but may not look the same, e.g. $\frac{1}{2}$ and $\frac{2}{4}$

## Supporting understanding
In Unit 17, children explored equivalence of unit fractions, i.e. $\frac{1}{2}$, $\frac{1}{3}$, $\frac{1}{4}$ and $\frac{1}{5}$.

Through previous work they will also be aware of equivalents for one whole, e.g. $\frac{3}{3}$ or $\frac{6}{6}$, shown here:

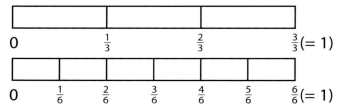

The fraction bar images, as used previously, will support the transition to fractions and equivalent fractions on the number line.

## Finding equivalents of familiar non-unit fractions
Children will begin to explore equivalents of fractions such as $\frac{3}{4}$, $\frac{2}{3}$ and $\frac{3}{5}$. All of these are already in their simplest form.

It is important that children recognise fraction bars that go together and relate these to multiples, e.g. quarters and eighths, thirds and sixths, fifths and tenths.

They should be able to explain that for every $\frac{1}{4}$ there are two lots of $\frac{1}{8}$, or $\frac{2}{8}$. This means that for $\frac{3}{4}$ there are three lots of $\frac{2}{8}$, or $\frac{6}{8}$.

### ANSWERS
**Task A:** $\frac{2}{6}$ and $\frac{3}{9}$; $\frac{4}{12}$ is the same as $\frac{1}{3}$

**Task B:** $\frac{2}{3}$, $\frac{4}{6}$, $\frac{6}{9}$, $\frac{8}{12}$, $\frac{10}{15}$; number line also showing $\frac{1}{3}$ ($\frac{2}{6}$, $\frac{3}{9}$, etc.) and one whole as $\frac{3}{3}$, $\frac{6}{6}$, etc.

**Challenge:** Extend number line and show fraction as $1\frac{2}{3}$, $1\frac{4}{6}$, etc.

**Task C:** $\frac{3}{5}$, $\frac{6}{10}$, $\frac{9}{15}$, $\frac{12}{20}$, $\frac{15}{25}$; number line also showing $\frac{1}{5}$ ($\frac{2}{10}$, $\frac{3}{15}$, etc.) and one whole as $\frac{5}{5}$, $\frac{10}{10}$, etc.

**Challenge:** Include $\frac{2}{5}$, $\frac{4}{10}$, $\frac{6}{15}$ and then $\frac{4}{5}$, $\frac{8}{10}$, $\frac{12}{15}$ on the number line; extend number line and show fraction as $1\frac{2}{5}$, $1\frac{4}{10}$, etc.

## In the classroom

Revisit the fractions and fraction bars that are equivalent to $\frac{1}{4}$ and ask children to describe the relationship between the numerator and denominator (as in Unit 17).

Look in more detail at the denominators: $\frac{1}{4}$, $\frac{2}{8}$, $\frac{3}{12}$. Pose these, or similar, questions for different groups to consider:

- *What do you notice?* (All are multiples of 4.)
- *What is the next fraction in the sequence? Why?*
- *Why would a fraction with the denominator 15 not be in my string of equivalents for $\frac{1}{4}$?*

*How can we use our fraction bars and what we now know about the denominators of equivalent fractions of $\frac{1}{4}$ to help us find equivalents for $\frac{3}{4}$?*

Compare fraction bars for quarters and eighths to establish that $\frac{6}{8}$ is equivalent to $\frac{3}{4}$ because for every one quarter there are two eighths. Use this language: *'For every $\frac{1}{4}$ there are $\frac{2}{8}$ so $\frac{6}{8}$ is equivalent to $\frac{3}{4}$'.*

As in previous units, model the transition of fraction bars to fractions on a number line. We can now place equivalent fractions for $\frac{1}{4}$ and $\frac{3}{4}$ on the number line.

Pose these, or similar, questions for different groups to consider:

- *Where should we place $\frac{1}{2}$ on the number line? How many **quarters** is this? And **eighths**?*
- *One whole is also on our number line. How can we write this in **quarters** and **eighths**?*
- *We know that $\frac{3}{12}$ is equivalent to $\frac{1}{4}$. How can we use this to find an equivalent for $\frac{3}{4}$?*

# Task A (Independent task)

You will need a set of fraction bars.

- Find the fraction bar that shows thirds.
- Find other fractions that are worth the same as $\frac{1}{3}$.
- Write them down as $\frac{1}{3} = $ ____ .
- Practise using this language each time:

> For every $\frac{1}{3}$ there are ____ so ____ is equivalent to $\frac{1}{3}$. They both are worth the same fraction of a whole.

Look at this new fraction bar. What fraction is the same as $\frac{1}{3}$?

# Task B (Guided learning with an adult)

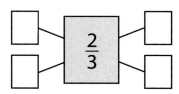

> For every $\frac{1}{3}$ there are ____ so ____ is equivalent to $\frac{2}{3}$.

- Find the fraction bar to match the denominator.
- Decide what other fraction bars will help you find equivalents for your fraction.
- Use the language to help you and then write the equivalents on the diagram.
- Now decide how your multiplication tables can help you find other equivalent fractions.
- Place all your equivalent fractions on a number line. Remember to show equivalents for $\frac{1}{3}$ and one whole.

**Challenge:** Where would you place an equivalent for $1\frac{2}{3}$?

# Task C (Independent task)

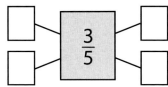

> For every $\frac{1}{5}$ there are ____ so ____ is equivalent to $\frac{3}{5}$.

- Use a fraction bar or draw an image of your own to show $\frac{3}{5}$.
- Decide what other denominators will help you find equivalents for your fraction.
- Use the language to help you and then write the equivalents on the diagram.
- Now decide how your multiplication tables can help you find other equivalent fractions.
- Place all your equivalent fractions on a number line. Remember to show equivalents for $\frac{1}{5}$ and one whole.

**Challenge:** Can you use what you know to place any equivalents for $\frac{2}{5}$ or $\frac{4}{5}$ on your number line? Can you place any equivalents for $1\frac{2}{5}$?

# Fractions as operators and division (1)

## National Curriculum link:

[Non-statutory guidance] Understand the relation between unit fractions as operators (fractions of), and division by integers.

## Year 3 pupils should already know that:

- Finding a half is the same as dividing into or by two
- Finding a quarter is the same as dividing into or by four
- Finding a quarter is the same as finding a half and then finding half again

## Supporting understanding

It is vital for children to recognise the relationship between fractions and division if they are to secure understanding.

In Unit 9, the following images were introduced to help develop understanding of finding fractions of amounts.

$\frac{1}{4}$ of 20 or 20 ÷ 4

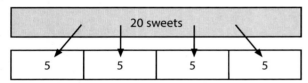

$\frac{1}{5}$ of 20 or 20 ÷ 5

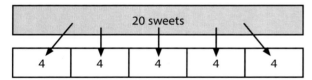

## Finding halves and quarters

One of the most common forms of division in the primary phases is halving. Children should be secure with the relationship between this and dividing into or by two.

Partitioning numbers to aid halving is key, particularly where numbers to be halved are odd amounts of tens, e.g. 90, or hundreds, e.g. 700.

Folding fraction strips in half and in half again also secures the concept that we can find a quarter by halving and halving again.

**ANSWERS**
**Task A: 1)** $\frac{1}{2}$ of 16 = 8 or 16 ÷ 2 **2)** $\frac{1}{2}$ of 22 = 11 or 22 ÷ 2 **3)** $\frac{1}{4}$ of 16 = 4 or 16 ÷ 4 **4)** $\frac{1}{3}$ of 12 = 4 or 12 ÷ 3 **5)** Fraction bars showing 9 divided into three parts with 3 in each
**Task B: 1)** $\frac{1}{5}$ of 30 = 6 or 30 ÷ 5 **2)** $\frac{1}{6}$ of 24 = 4 or 24 ÷ 6
**3)** Fraction bars showing 21 divided into three parts with 7 in each
**4)** Fraction bars showing 24 divided into four parts with 6 in each
**5)** Fraction bars showing 25 divided into five parts with 5 in each
**Task C: 1)** $\frac{1}{6}$ of 36 = 6 or 36 ÷ 6 **2)** $\frac{1}{7}$ of 28 = 4 or 28 ÷ 7
**3)** Fraction bars showing 40 divided into eight parts with 5 in each
**4)** Fraction bars showing 42 divided into six parts with 7 in each
**5)** Fraction bars showing 60 divided into ten parts with 6 in each
**6)** 27 **7)** 3 **8)** $\frac{1}{4}$

## In the classroom

Revisit the key point that we can use halving to help us divide by 2 by posing the question:

*What strategies can I use to help me divide these numbers by 2?* (E.g. 8 ÷ 2, 18 ÷ 2, 38 ÷ 2.)

Establish that we can find half of 8, half of 18 and half of 38. Children should quickly practise methods of halving.

Rewrite the calculation 18 ÷ 2 = 9 as $\frac{1}{2}$ of 18 = 9.

Other calculations can be written in the same way.

Make clear the link between the divisor (2) and the value of the denominator (2).

Using the image of 20 sweets divided by 4 (shown left), discuss with children which calculations this represents.

Establish that it shows $\frac{1}{4}$ of 20 or 20 ÷ 4. Again, note that the divisor (4) and the denominator in the fraction (4) are the same.

Revisit the key point that we can find a quarter by halving and halving again.

Pose these, or similar, questions for different groups to consider:

- *What calculation does this image represent?* (Provide another image, e.g. 12 ÷ 4 or 20 ÷ 2.)

- *What image could I draw to represent 15 ÷ 3? How can I write this calculation using fractions?*

- *What image could I draw to represent $\frac{1}{5}$ of 15? How can I write this calculation using division?*

Izzy drew this image to represent $\frac{1}{6}$ of 18:

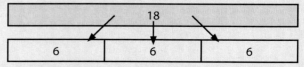

What do you think? Discuss why Izzy's image represents thirds not sixths.

# Task A (Independent task)

What calculations do these images show?
Write the division (÷) and fraction calculation each time.

1)
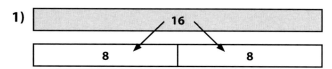

2)
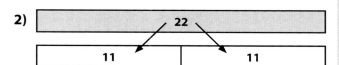

3)
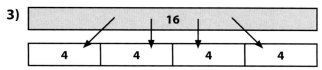

4)
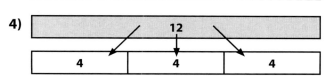

**5)** What image would you draw for $9 \div 3$ or $\frac{1}{3}$ of 9?

# Task B (Independent task)

What calculations do these images show?
Write the division (÷) and fraction calculation each time.

1)
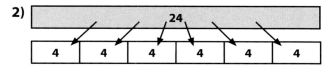

2)

Draw images for the following calculations.

**3)** $21 \div 3$

**4)** $\frac{1}{4}$ of 24

**5)** $\frac{1}{5}$ of 25

# Task C (Independent task)

What calculations do these images show?

1)
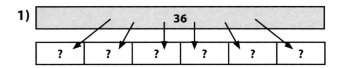

2)
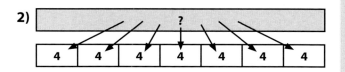

Draw images for the following calculations.

**3)** $\frac{1}{8}$ of 40

**4)** $42 \div 6$

**5)** $\frac{1}{10}$ of 60

Copy and complete the following.

**6)** $\frac{1}{9}$ of _____ = 3

**7)** $27 \div$ _____ = 9

**8)** _____ of 48 = 12

# UNIT 20  Fractions as operators and division (2)

## National Curriculum link:

[Non-statutory guidance] Understand the relation between unit fractions as operators (fractions of), and division by integers.

## Year 3 pupils should already know that:

- Finding a half is the same as dividing into or by two
- Finding a quarter is the same as dividing into or by four
- Finding a unit fraction of an amount is the same as dividing the amount by the value of the denominator

## Supporting understanding

In Unit 19, children looked at the relationship between finding a fraction of an amount and division.

In the independent tasks, children drew and described images to represent calculations, e.g. $\frac{1}{3}$ of 12 and 12 ÷ 3.

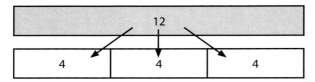

A key point to be secured is that the value of the denominator determines the divisor in the related division calculation, e.g. in the fraction $\frac{1}{5}$, the value of the denominator is 5 (it can be described as one whole divided into five equal parts) so to find $\frac{1}{5}$ of an amount (whole), we must divide by 5.

## Using language structures

Making links using language structures also reinforces this relationship.

> One **quarter** of **20** is **5** because **20** divided by **4** is **5**.

> One **fifth** of **20** is **4** because **20** divided by **5** is **4**.

Language should be modelled by teachers and other adults and practised by children.

### ANSWERS

**Task A:** E.g. pick 15 metres and find $\frac{1}{5}$ of it; record as $\frac{1}{5}$ of 15 metres and 15 metres ÷ 5 = 3 metres

**Task B:** E.g. roll 6 to make $\frac{1}{6}$; pick 18 metres and find $\frac{1}{6}$ of it; record as $\frac{1}{6}$ of 18 metres and 18 metres ÷ 6 = 3 metres

**Task C:** E.g. roll 3 to make $\frac{1}{3}$; pick 48 metres and find $\frac{1}{3}$ of it; record as $\frac{1}{3}$ of 48 metres and 48 metres ÷ 3 = 16 metres

## In the classroom

Revisit the key point that when we find a fraction of an amount, it is the same as dividing the amount by the value of the denominator, e.g. $\frac{1}{4}$ of 12 metres, $\frac{1}{5}$ of 20 metres, $\frac{1}{8}$ of 32 metres.

Use this language: 'How can we write each of these as a division?'

Consider $\frac{1}{5}$ of 20 metres.

Use this language: 'What is $\frac{1}{5}$ of 20 metres? What would a fraction bar image look like?'

Use this language: 'One fifth of 20 metres is 4 metres because 20 divided by 5 is 4.'

Ask children to practise using this language to make sense of $\frac{1}{5}$ of 25 metres or any of the fractions they were thinking about earlier.

Pose these, or similar, questions for different groups to consider:

- What is $\frac{1}{5}$ of 10 metres?
- Would you rather find $\frac{1}{5}$ of 10 metres or $\frac{1}{5}$ of 12 metres? Why?
- What other measurements would it be easy to find $\frac{1}{5}$ of?
- What do you notice about them?

Establish that it is easier to find $\frac{1}{5}$ of a multiple of 5 as this is the same as dividing a number by 5. Numbers in the 5 times table divide exactly by 5 with no remainders.

Discuss the numbers that are easy to divide by 2 (find $\frac{1}{2}$ of), by 4 (find $\frac{1}{4}$ of) or by 6 (find $\frac{1}{6}$ of).

Be clear that we can find fractions of other numbers or metres, e.g. $\frac{1}{2}$ of 13 or $\frac{1}{5}$ of 12, but the answers will not be whole numbers.

# Task A (Independent task or guided learning with an adult)

| 20 metres | 15 metres | 16 metres |
|-----------|-----------|-----------|
| 24 metres | 12 metres | |

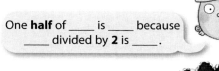

One **half** of _____ is _____ because _____ divided by **2** is _____.

One **quarter** of _____ is _____ because _____ divided by **4** is _____.

1) Choose a number of metres from the grid above.
2) What multiplication table is this number in? Is it in more than one?
3) Decide to find $\frac{1}{2}$, $\frac{1}{4}$ or $\frac{1}{5}$ of the number.
4) Use the language in the speech bubbles to help you.
5) Record your calculation as a fraction and as a division (÷).

One **fifth** of _____ is _____ because _____ divided by **5** is _____.

**Challenge:** Use the blank box for a number of metres of your choice.

# Task B (Independent task)

| 40 metres | 12 metres | 24 metres |
|-----------|-----------|-----------|
| 25 metres | 18 metres | 30 metres |
| 16 metres | 36 metres | |

One _____ of _____ is _____ because _____ divided by _____ is _____.

1) Roll the dice to make a fraction, e.g. roll a 3 to make $\frac{1}{3}$, roll a 1 to make $\frac{1}{10}$.
2) Thinking about multiplication tables, choose a number of metres from the grid.
3) Find the fraction of this amount.
4) Use the language in the speech bubble to help you.
5) Record your calculation as a fraction and as a division (÷).

**Challenge:** Use the blank box for a number of metres of your choice.

# Task C (Independent task)

| 90 metres | 42 metres | 24 metres |
|-----------|-----------|-----------|
| 45 metres | 27 metres | 48 metres |
| 60 metres | 36 metres | |

One _____ of _____ is _____ because _____ divided by _____ is _____.

1) Roll the dice to make a fraction, e.g. roll a 3 to make $\frac{1}{3}$, roll a 1 to make $\frac{1}{10}$.
2) Thinking about multiplication tables, choose a number of metres from the grid.
3) Find the fraction of this amount.
4) Use the language in the speech bubble to help you.
5) Record your calculation as a fraction and as a division (÷).

**Challenge:** Use the blank box for a number of your choice.

# UNIT 21  Solving problems about fractions (1)

## National Curriculum link:
Recognise and show, using diagrams, equivalent fractions with small denominators.

## Year 3 pupils should already know that:
- Fractions are numbers in their own right and have a place on the number line
- It is easy to compare and calculate (+ and −) with fractions that have the same denominator
- Some fractions may look different but have the same value, e.g. $\frac{5}{10}$ and $\frac{1}{2}$
- Fractions as operators are related to division

## Supporting understanding

In previous units, children have been exploring ordering fractions and finding equivalent fractions.

In this unit, the problem requires children to use this knowledge to help them make decisions about making fractions.

Images like the number line can be used to help order fractions. Multiplication facts and other images should be used to support children to identify sets of equivalent fractions. Remember that we can also look for equivalent fractions beyond 1.

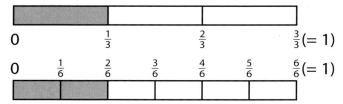

## Problem solving

It is important that children have plenty of opportunities to apply knowledge and skills.

This not only secures understanding but also provides evidence of learning.

To be successful, children must first make sense of the problem and find a starting point.

Encourage children to tell the story of the problem, role-play it or sketch something that helps them make sense of it.

As teachers, we need to model how to be a problem solver and show children how to find starting points.

## In the classroom

Introduce the problem that will be developed throughout the lesson:

- *Children in Class 3 are playing different games.*
- *Jade and Izzy each have six number cards.*

| Jade | 1 | 2 | 3 | 4 | 5 | 6 |
|------|---|---|---|---|---|---|

| Izzy | 2 | 4 | 6 | 8 | 10 | 12 |
|------|---|---|---|---|----|----|

*They each use pairs of number cards to make different fractions, e.g. Jade can use 1 and 2 to make $\frac{1}{2}$.*

Ask different groups to work on the possible fractions that can be made by Jade or Izzy. Numbers can be used more than once.

Challenge more able children to make as many fractions as they can from Izzy's numbers that are greater than one half.

Collect a range of fractions for both Jade and Izzy. Discuss ways to place some of Jade's fractions in order on a number line.

Consider Izzy's fractions. Ask the more able children to contribute their ideas to help place some fractions in order.

*We can also use the cards to make fractions that are greater than 1, e.g. for Jade, $2\frac{3}{4}$ using the 2, 3 and 4 cards.*

*Some of the fractions that Jade made had the same value as some of Izzy's fractions, but they did not look the same.*

Ask children to work on tasks to find possible solutions.

### ANSWERS
**Task A: 1)** $\frac{2}{4}, \frac{4}{8}, \frac{6}{12}$ **2)** $\frac{2}{8}$ **3)** Yes, Jade $\frac{3}{4}$ and Izzy $\frac{6}{8}$
**Task B: 1)** $\frac{6}{8}$ **2)** $\frac{2}{6}$ and $\frac{4}{12}$ **3)** $\frac{1}{2}$ or $\frac{2}{4}$ or $\frac{3}{6}$ (Jade) and $\frac{2}{4}, \frac{4}{8}, \frac{6}{12}$ (Izzy); $\frac{2}{3}$
or $\frac{4}{6}$ (Jade) and $\frac{4}{6}, \frac{8}{12}$ (Izzy), $\frac{1}{5}$ (Jade) and $\frac{2}{10}$ (Izzy); $\frac{2}{5}$ (Jade) and $\frac{4}{10}$
(Izzy), etc. **4)** Izzy does not have a 1 so she cannot make $\frac{1}{10}$, she
does not have 20 so cannot make $\frac{2}{20}$ **5)** $1\frac{2}{4}$ and $1\frac{3}{6}$
**Task C: 1)** $\frac{4}{10}$ **2)** $\frac{4}{6}$ and $\frac{8}{12}$ **3)** As for Task B question 3 **4)** Children's
choices **5)** The 1, 3 and 4 for $1\frac{3}{4}$

# Task A  (Independent task or guided learning with an adult)

Jade | 1 | 2 | 3 | 4 | 5 | 6

Izzy | 2 | 4 | 6 | 8 | 10 | 12

Here are two of the fractions that Jade made:

$\frac{1}{2}$ and $\frac{1}{4}$

1) What fractions could Izzy have made that have the same value as $\frac{1}{2}$?

2) What fractions could Izzy have made that have the same value as $\frac{1}{4}$?

3) Could both Jade and Izzy have made the fraction $\frac{3}{4}$? Remember that they may not look the same!

# Task B  (Independent task or guided learning with an adult)

Jade | 1 | 2 | 3 | 4 | 5 | 6

Izzy | 2 | 4 | 6 | 8 | 10 | 12

Here are two of the fractions that Jade made:

$\frac{3}{4}$ and $\frac{1}{3}$

1) What fractions could Izzy have made that have the same value as $\frac{3}{4}$?

2) What fractions could Izzy have made that have the same value as $\frac{1}{3}$?

3) What other equivalent fractions could Izzy and Jade have made?

4) How can you prove that Izzy cannot have made a fraction equivalent to $\frac{1}{10}$?

5) What fractions could Jade have made that are equivalent to $1\frac{1}{2}$?

# Task C  (Independent task)

Jade | 1 | 2 | 3 | 4 | 5 | 6 | 

Izzy | 2 | 4 | 6 | 8 | 10 | 12 | 

Here are two of the fractions that Jade made:

$\frac{2}{3}$ and $\frac{2}{5}$

1) What fractions could Izzy have made that have the same value as $\frac{2}{5}$?

2) What fractions could Izzy have made that have the same value as $\frac{2}{3}$?

3) What other equivalent fractions could Izzy and Jade have made?

4) Both Jade and Izzy also have a blank card. Choose two different numbers for the cards to help make other sets of equivalent fractions.

5) How can Jade use her cards to make a fraction equal to $1\frac{6}{8}$?

# Solving problems about fractions (2)

UNIT 22

## National Curriculum link:

Recognise and show, using diagrams, equivalent fractions with small denominators.

## Year 3 pupils should already know that:

- Fractions are numbers in their own right and have a place on the number line
- It is easy to compare and calculate (+ and –) with fractions that have the same denominator
- Some fractions may look different but have the same value, e.g. $\frac{5}{10}$ and $\frac{1}{2}$
- Fractions as operators are related to division

## Supporting understanding

Remember that throughout this book, several different images have been used to support children with their work on fractions.

In this unit, a chocolate bar image will be useful as it is also the context of the problem.

Children should look for other images in everyday life that support understanding of fractions.

## Solving problems with more than one solution

Children should be encouraged to look for more than one solution and therefore must have access to a range of problems that require this.

More able children, in particular, are less inclined to search for additional solutions when one has already been found.

They should also be challenged with problems where a solution is not possible or to look for counterexamples once a rule has been found.

As teachers, we should also model making generalisations and show children how to organise their thinking and results, and consider more than one solution.

### ANSWERS

**Task A:** E.g. Alice $\frac{1}{6}$ of 12 = 2, Jamie $\frac{1}{4}$ of 12 = 3 and Izzy $\frac{1}{2}$ of 12 = 6
**Challenge:** E.g. Alice eats 3 pieces, which is $\frac{1}{4}$ of the bar; Jamie then eats $\frac{1}{3}$ and Izzy $\frac{1}{2}$
**Task B: 1)** E.g. for a ten-piece bar, Tom and Sami eat $\frac{5}{10}$ in total; $\frac{3}{10}$ $+ \frac{2}{10} = \frac{5}{10}$ **2)** $\frac{5}{6}$, $\frac{5}{8}$, $\frac{5}{10}$, $\frac{5}{12}$ **3)** The least number of pieces possible is six as we know the number is even and Tom and Sami ate five parts **4)** $\frac{7}{12}$ are left because Tom and Sami ate $\frac{5}{12}$ in total; $\frac{7}{12} + \frac{5}{12} = \frac{12}{12}$
**Task C:** Cool Choc had either seven or eight pieces: $\frac{3}{7}$ (Sally) + $\frac{3}{7}$ (Ishmal) + $\frac{1}{7}$ (Ami) or $\frac{3}{8}$ (Sally) + $\frac{4}{8}$ (Ishmal) + $\frac{1}{8}$ (Ami); Chocolate Chunk had either eleven or twelve pieces (when there were eight or seven pieces of Cool Choc, respectively): $\frac{3}{11}$ (Sally) + $\frac{3}{11}$ (Ishmal) $+ \frac{5}{11}$ (remaining) or $\frac{3}{12}$ (Sally) + $\frac{4}{12}$ (Ishmal) + $\frac{5}{12}$ (remaining); Choco had nine pieces: $\frac{3}{9}$ (Sally) + $\frac{1}{9}$ (Ishmal) + $\frac{3}{9}$ (Ami) + $\frac{2}{9}$ (remaining)

## In the classroom

Introduce the problem that will be developed throughout the lesson. Use this language: *The local shop sells different makes of chocolate bars: Chip Choc, Chocolate Chunk, Crispy Choc and more! Here is the Crispy Choc bar.*

- *What different fractions of this bar will it be easy to calculate? Why?*
- *How could we write these fractions using division?*

*Jamie, Alice and Izzy each buy a Crispy Choc bar. They all eat some of their chocolate bar. Jamie eats more of his bar than Alice but less than Izzy.*

Pose these, or similar, questions for different groups to consider:

- *If Alice ate $\frac{1}{4}$, how many pieces has she eaten?*
- *Can Alice have eaten $\frac{6}{12}$ and Jamie $\frac{1}{2}$? Why not?*
- *What different fractions of the bar could each child have eaten? How do you know?*
- *What fraction shows the fewest pieces that Alice could have eaten?*

Record some different possibilities in a table, e.g:

| Alice | Jamie | Izzy |
|---|---|---|
| $\frac{1}{12}$ of 12 = 1 | $\frac{1}{6}$ of 12 = 2 | $\frac{1}{4}$ of 12 = 3 |
| $\frac{1}{12}$ of 12 = 1 | $\frac{1}{4}$ of 12 = 3 | $\frac{1}{3}$ of 12 = 4 |

Establish that there are more possibilities.

Ask children to look at problems about the other chocolate bars in the shop. Task A continues with the Crispy Choc problem.

## Task **A** (Independent task or guided learning with an adult)

Remember that in the problem Jamie eats more of his bar than Alice but less than Izzy.

Use what you already know to find some more possible solutions.

**Crispy Choc**

| Alice | Jamie | Izzy |
|---|---|---|
| $\frac{1}{12}$ of 12 = 1 | $\frac{1}{6}$ of 12 = 2 | $\frac{1}{4}$ of 12 = 3 |
| $\frac{1}{12}$ of 12 = 1 | $\frac{1}{4}$ of 12 = 3 | $\frac{1}{3}$ of 12 = 4 |
| | | |
| | | |
| | | |

**Challenge:** Alice eats more than two pieces. What fraction of her bar could she have eaten?

What do you now know about the fractions eaten by Jamie and Izzy?

## Task **B** (Independent task or guided learning with an adult)

A bar of Chip Choc has an even number of pieces. It has less than 13 pieces.

Tom eats three pieces and Sami eats two pieces.

**1)** Choose a possible number of pieces for the whole bar of Chip Choc.
  - Find the fraction of the whole bar eaten by Tom and Sami.
  - Write the calculation you used.

**2)** Now find all possibilities.

**3)** Explain what you know about the least possible number of pieces in a Chip Choc bar.

**4)** What fraction of the bar is left if the whole bar had 12 pieces? How do you know?

## Task **C** (Guided learning with an adult)

Sally, Ishmal and Ami have three chocolate bars between them.

Use the clues to find out how many pieces of chocolate are in each whole bar and what fraction of each bar was eaten by Sally, Ishmal or Ami.

- Sally ate three pieces from each of the chocolate bars.
- Ishmal ate only one piece of Choco, but he also ate three pieces from a second bar and four pieces from the last bar.
- Ami ate the last piece of Cool Choc and three pieces of Choco.
- There are two pieces of Choco and five pieces of Chocolate Chunk left.

Prove your solution by showing the fractions and calculations you have used.

There is more than one solution!

# RISING ★ STARS
# Maths

## Supporting schools through curriculum change

### www.risingstars-uk.com/maths

# Fluency with Fractions

## TEACHER'S GUIDE

Steph King

YEAR 4

**Rising Stars UK Ltd**
**7 Hatchers Mews, Bermondsey Street, London, SE1 3GS**

**www.risingstars-uk.com**

Published 2014
Reprinted 2014, 2015
Text, design and layout © Rising Stars UK Ltd.

The right of Steph King to be identified as the author of this work has been asserted by her in accordance with the Copyright, Design and Patents Act 1998.

**Author:** Steph King
**Consultant:** Cherri Moseley
**Publisher:** Fiona Lazenby
**Project Manager:** Debbie Allen
**Editorial:** Katharine Timberlake, Kate Manson
**Cover design:** Burville-Riley Partnership
**Design:** Marc Burville-Riley
**Typesetting:** Fakenham Prepress Solutions
**Illustrations:** Louise Forshaw / Advocate Art, Richard and Benjamin,
     Fakenham Prepress Solutions
**CD-ROM development:** Alex Morris

British Library Cataloguing in Publication Data.
A CIP record for this book is available from the British Library.

ISBN: 978-1-78339-183-7

Printed by: Ashford Colour Press Ltd, Gosport, Hants

MIX
Paper from
responsible sources
FSC
www.fsc.org    FSC® C011748

# Contents

## Fractions in the 2014 National Curriculum

The National Curriculum aims to ensure that all pupils become fluent in the fundamentals of mathematics, can reason mathematically and can solve problems by applying their mathematics. With a significant shift in expectations in the 2014 Programme of Study, children are required to work with and calculate using a range of fractions at an earlier stage. Achieving fluency will depend on developing conceptual understanding through a variety of practical and contextual opportunities.

## Statutory requirements and non-statutory guidance

At first glance, the statutory requirements for the Fractions domain for younger children may not appear to be that extensive. However, it is important to note that each 'objective' is made up of a range of different skills and knowledge that need to be addressed. We must remember that mastery of one aspect does not necessarily imply mastery of another.

The Programme of Study also provides non-statutory guidance that helps to clarify, secure and extend learning in each domain to best prepare children for the next stage of mathematical development. Units in this *Fluency with Fractions* series, therefore, also address some aspects of the non-statutory guidance. These objectives are flagged where applicable.

## Fractions across the domains

Learning about fractions is not exclusive to the Fractions domain in the Programme of Study. Conceptual understanding of fractions is also addressed and applied through work on time, turns, angles and through many other aspects of measurement, geometry and also statistics. We must also remember to continue to practise and extend learning from previous year groups even if a concept is not explicitly covered in the Programme of Study for the current year group. The other domains provide useful opportunities for this.

## Making the links: decimals, percentages, ratio and proportion

Children will first experience decimals in the context of measurement. However, security with place value is vital if they are to truly understand how the position of a digit on either side of the decimal point determines its size. Place value charts and grids are used in this series of books to continue to reinforce this concept and to help children make sense of tenths, hundredths and thousandths.

As children progress through the Programmes of Study, they will later meet percentages. Recognising that a fraction such as $\frac{25}{100}$ can be written as $25 \div 100$, and therefore as 0.25, will help make the connection to 25%.

Finding and identifying equivalent fractions will later pave the way for understanding equivalent ratios.

For this reason, within the *Fluency with Fractions* series, the Year 4 book includes work on decimals, Year 5 includes percentages and Year 6 goes on to incorporate ratio and proportion.

## Developing conceptual understanding through the use of resources

Children should be given opportunities to develop conceptual understanding through a range of practical experiences and the use of visual representations to help them make sense of fractions. Manipulatives, such as Base 10 apparatus, cubes and counters, along with other resources, should be used skilfully to model concepts and provide a reference point to help children make connections for future learning. Moving in this way from concrete resources to pictorial representations to symbolic notation for fractions will help to secure conceptual understanding.

## Developing mathematical language

Language is often cited as a barrier to learning, so it is important to model technical vocabulary that helps children to use it confidently and to help them explain their mathematical thinking and reasoning. Appropriate language structures are suggested throughout the Units.

# Using representations to support understanding

Fractions is a part of mathematics that children often find more difficult to learn than other areas. This, in turn, is often the result of teachers finding the concepts more difficult to teach. We need to help children to see what we mean and make links to other familiar representations that they know, e.g. number lines.

Historically, images to support the teaching of fractions have tended to be related to real-life examples that children see 'cut-up' and shared. Pizzas, cakes and chocolate are examples of this. Although these representations are valuable (particularly circular images that will later inform work on pie charts), it is the linear image that directly relates to the number line that will support the transition of concrete to abstract when counting and calculating.

Throughout the *Fluency with Fractions* resources, fraction bar images are used in each year level to introduce the concept of fractions as equal parts of a whole, equivalence, counting (linked to the number line) and calculating.

The following diagrams provide a few generic examples to illustrate how different images are used. Templates for some useful images are provided on the accompanying CD-ROM.

- Fractions as equal parts of one whole.

- Linking fractions to counting on a number line.

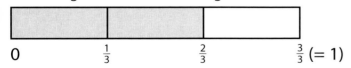

- Counting on the number line to reinforce that fractions are numbers in their own right. Counting paves the way for calculating.

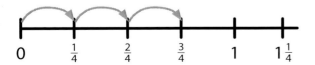

- Developing a range of images to explore equivalent fractions.

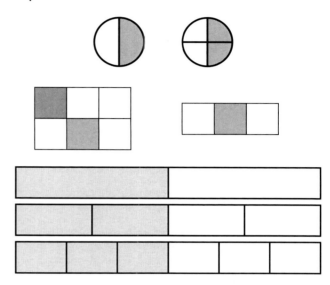

- Comparing fractions on a number line.

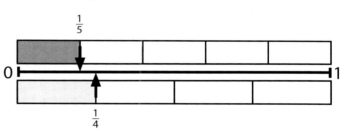

- Using fraction bars to support early calculation of fractions of amounts.

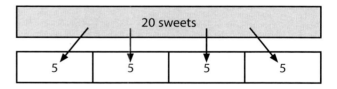

- Using fraction bars to support identifying an amount represented by a fraction.

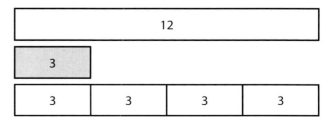

# How to use this book

The Units in this book support the development of conceptual understanding of fractions and are intended to be used to introduce concepts. Learning should be practised and revisited regularly using other resources to consolidate and deepen understanding.

Each Unit within the books is structured in the same way, providing guidance to support teachers and an example teaching sequence.

Tasks can be used as suggested or adapted accordingly to meet the needs of each setting. Guided learning provides an opportunity for the adult to take learning forward with a group or to take part in an activity that has a greater problem-solving element and where language may be more demanding. Additional editable resource sheets are provided on the accompanying CD-ROM to support this.

Bold text shows the link to the NC objectives or the non-statutory guidance.

Please check that prior learning is in place before working on this unit.

This section helps teachers to make connections through the use of visual representations and language structures.

Tasks may be directed at the teacher to run the activity with children as guided learning; directed at the teacher to explain the activity to children to do independently; or directed at children to be photocopied and given out for independent work. Tasks increase in level of difficulty.

Task B is aimed at the majority of children who will progress at the expected rate.

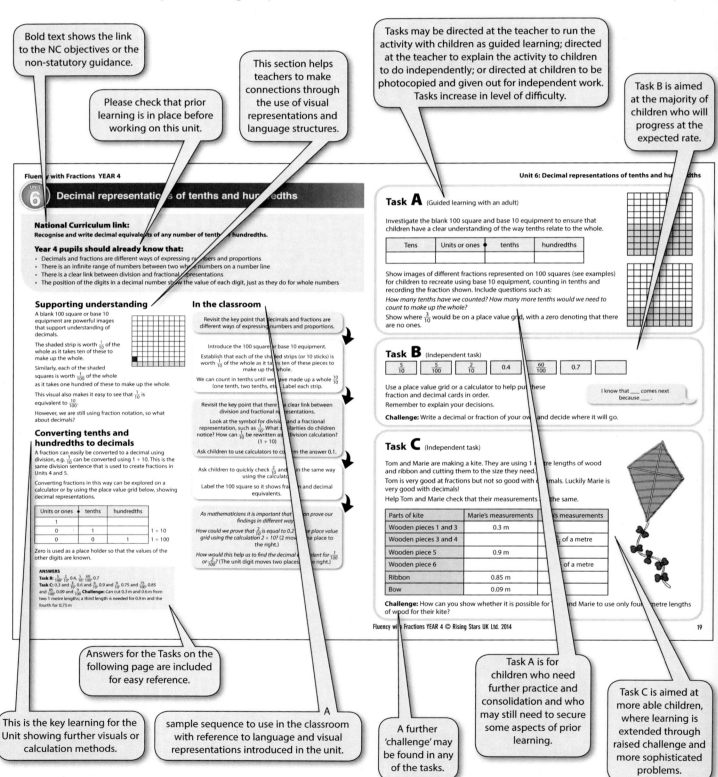

Answers for the Tasks on the following page are included for easy reference.

This is the key learning for the Unit showing further visuals or calculation methods.

sample sequence to use in the classroom with reference to language and visual representations introduced in the unit.

A further 'challenge' may be found in any of the tasks.

Task A is for children who need further practice and consolidation and who may still need to secure some aspects of prior learning.

Task C is aimed at more able children, where learning is extended through raised challenge and more sophisticated problems.

# Curriculum mapping grid

The grid below shows in which Units objectives from the 2014 National Curriculum Programme of Study for Year 4 are covered. Note that objectives are revisited regularly and learning progressed in subsequent units. In the National Curriculum link section of each Unit, bold text is used to indicate which specific part of the overarching objective is addressed within the Unit, since objectives often cover a range of different knowledge and skills (particularly for younger age groups).

| Objectives \ Unit | 1 | 2 | 3 | 4 | 5 | 6 | 7 | 8 | 9 | 10 | 11 | 12 | 13 | 14 | 15 | 16 | 17 | 18 | 19 | 20 | 21 | 22 |
|---|---|---|---|---|---|---|---|---|---|---|---|---|---|---|---|---|---|---|---|---|---|---|
| Extend the use of the number line to connect fractions, numbers and measures. | ✓ | | | | | | | | | | | | | | | | | | | | | |
| Practise counting using simple fractions and decimals, both forwards and backwards. | ✓ | | | | | | | | | | | | ✓ | | | | | | | | | |
| Count up and down in hundredths; recognise that hundredths arise when dividing an object by one hundred and dividing tenths by ten. | | ✓ | ✓ | | | | | | | | | | | | | | | | | | | |
| Find the effect of dividing a one- or two-digit number by 10 and 100, identifying the value of the digits in the answer as ones, tenths and hundredths. | | | | ✓ | ✓ | | | | | | | | | | | | | | | | | |
| Recognise and write decimal equivalents of any number of tenths or hundredths. | | | | | | ✓ | | | | | | | | | | | | | | | | |
| Recognise and show, using diagrams, families of common equivalent fractions. | | | | | | | ✓ | ✓ | | | | | | | | | | | | | | |
| Recognise and write decimal equivalents to $\frac{1}{4}, \frac{1}{2}, \frac{3}{4}$. | | | | | | | | | ✓ | | | | | | | | | | | | | |
| Practise counting using simple fractions and decimals, both forwards and backwards. | | | | | | | | | | ✓ | | | | | | | | | | | | |
| Round decimals with one decimal place to the nearest whole number. | | | | | | | | | | | ✓ | | | | | | | | | | | |
| Compare numbers with the same number of decimal places up to two decimal places. | | | | | | | | | | | | ✓ | | | | | | | | | | |
| Solve simple measure and money problems involving fractions and decimals to two decimal places. | | | | | | | | | | | | | ✓ | ✓ | | | | | | | ✓ | ✓ |
| Solve problems involving increasingly harder fractions to calculate quantities, and fractions to divide quantities, including non-unit fractions where the answer is a whole number. | | | | | | | | | | | | | | | ✓ | ✓ | ✓ | | | | | |
| Add and subtract fractions with the same denominator. | | | | | | | | | | | | | | | | | | ✓ | ✓ | ✓ | | |

# UNIT 1

# Fractions and the number line

## National Curriculum link:

[Non-statutory guidance] **Extend the use of the number line to connect fractions, numbers** and measures.
[Non-statutory guidance] **Practise counting using simple fractions** and decimals, **both forwards and backwards**

## Year 4 pupils should already know that:

- A fraction is a number in its own right and can be placed on the number line
- The denominator determines the number of equal parts the whole is divided into and the numerator shows how many of these equal parts are represented by the fraction, e.g. $\frac{1}{3}$, $\frac{2}{3}$ or $\frac{3}{3}$

## Supporting understanding

In Year 3, children counted in fraction steps to help secure understanding that fractions are numbers in their own right and can be placed on a number line.

They used images, such as fraction bars, to explore unit and non-unit fractions as parts (proportions) of the whole.

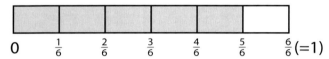

It is a fraction with **6** equal parts.
I have **5** of the parts. I have $\frac{5}{6}$.

Additional bars can be added to show fractions greater than 1.

## Fractions on the number line

We can show fractions made up of fraction steps on the number line. Here, each step has a value of $\frac{1}{6}$.

It is useful for children to count the fraction steps as they go to help prepare them for calculating with fractions, e.g. $\frac{1}{6}$, $\frac{2}{6}$, $\frac{3}{6}$, $\frac{4}{6}$, $\frac{5}{6}$.

The language can be developed for mixed numbers as e.g.: 'There are **2** wholes and a part of a whole. The fraction had **6** equal parts and I have **5** of them. I have **2** and $\frac{5}{6}$.'

### ANSWERS

**Task A:** A selection of number lines with fraction steps for fractions such as $\frac{3}{4}$, $\frac{3}{5}$, $\frac{4}{10}$, etc.

**Challenge:** 1) $\frac{1}{2}$, $\frac{2}{4}$, $\frac{4}{8}$, $\frac{5}{10}$ 2) $\frac{2}{2}$, $\frac{3}{3}$, $\frac{4}{4}$, $\frac{5}{5}$

**Task B:** A selection of number lines with fraction steps for fractions such as $\frac{3}{5}$, $\frac{4}{8}$, $\frac{7}{10}$, etc. 1) $\frac{4}{4}$, $\frac{5}{5}$, $\frac{7}{8}$, $\frac{9}{10}$ (if 9 chosen), etc. 2) $\frac{2}{6}$, $\frac{3}{9}$ (if 9 chosen), $\frac{4}{12}$ (if 12 chosen), etc. 3) $\frac{2}{10}$, children's choices

**Task C:** 1) $\frac{4}{6}$, $\frac{6}{9}$ (if 6 chosen), $\frac{10}{15}$ (if 10 and 15 chosen), etc. 2) $\frac{2}{6}$, $\frac{2}{8}$, $\frac{2}{9}$, etc., $\frac{3}{8}$, $\frac{3}{9}$, etc, $\frac{4}{9}$, etc, $\frac{5}{12}$ 3) $\frac{7}{6}$, number line to show 7 jumps of $\frac{1}{6}$ finishing at $\frac{7}{6}$ or $1\frac{1}{6}$

## In the classroom

Revisit the key point that the denominator determines the number of equal parts the whole is divided into.

Provide differentiated images for children to describe, including some that go beyond 1, for example:

Model the use of a number line to show the key point that fractions are numbers in their own right, e.g. $\frac{5}{6}$. They are also proportions (parts) of a whole.

Count in sixths and use the language structure modelled to the left for mixed numbers.

Count up to $1\frac{5}{6}$ to show that the fraction part of the number remains the same.

Invite children to draw similar number lines to represent the image they were describing previously.

Encourage them to count and use the language above.

Pose these, or similar, questions for different groups to consider about their number lines:

- *How many fraction steps have you counted?*
- *How many more do you need to count to reach 1? 2?*
- *Is your fraction larger or smaller than $\frac{1}{2}$? Or $1\frac{1}{2}$? How do you know?*

Present the following problem:

- *Izzy made four fraction steps along her number line.*
- *What fraction could this be?*
  Use this language: *'It could be … because … .'*

Record some of the suggestions for the possible fraction, e.g. $\frac{4}{4}$, $\frac{4}{5}$, $\frac{4}{6}$, $\frac{4}{7}$, $\frac{4}{8}$, $\frac{4}{9}$, etc. and ask different groups to consider the following ideas:

- *Which of these fractions is equal to or nearest to $1/\frac{1}{2}/0$?*
- *What would happen if Izzy made four steps of $\frac{1}{2}$ along her number line?*

# Task **A** (Independent task or guided learning with an adult)

Thinking carefully, choose a number for the numerator and another for the denominator to make a fraction.

- Use this language: '*It is a fraction with ___ equal parts. I have ___ of the parts. I have ___*' to describe your fraction.

Draw the number line to match your fraction.
Now make other fractions in the same way.

| Numerators | | |
|---|---|---|
| **1** | **2** | **3** |
| **4** | **5** | **6** |
| Denominators | | |
| **2** | **3** | **4** |
| **5** | **8** | **10** |

**Challenge:**

1) Are any of your fractions equal to a half? Which ones?   2) Can you make fractions equal to one whole?

# Task **B** (Independent task or guided learning with an adult)

Choose a number for the numerator and another for the denominator to make different fractions.

- Use this language: '*It is a fraction with ___ equal parts. I have ___ of the parts. I have ___*' to describe your fractions.

Draw the number lines to match your fractions.
Now use the ? for a numerator or denominator of your choice.

1) Which of your fractions are equal to one or are nearest to one?
2) Are any of your fractions equal to a third? Which ones?
3) Which is the smallest fraction and will be closest to zero?

| Numerators | | |
|---|---|---|
| **2** | **3** | **4** |
| **5** | **7** | **?** |
| Denominators | | |
| **4** | **5** | **6** |
| **8** | **10** | **?** |

**Challenge:**
Draw a number line to show the number $1\frac{7}{8}$.

# Task **C** (Independent task)

Choose numbers from the grid to make different fractions.
You can use the ? for a numerator or denominator of your choice.

- Use this language: '*There are ___ equal parts and I have ___ of them. I have ___*' to describe each fraction.

Draw the number lines to match your fractions.

1) Are any of your fractions equal to $\frac{2}{3}$? Which ones?
2) Which of your fractions will sit on the number line between zero and a half?
3) Zack made a fraction that was greater than one. He did not use either **?**.
   What fraction did he make?
   Draw the number line for this fraction.

| Numerators | | |
|---|---|---|
| **2** | **3** | **4** |
| **5** | **7** | **?** |
| Denominators | | |
| **6** | **8** | **9** |
| **10** | **12** | **?** |

# UNIT 2  Understanding and counting in hundredths

## National Curriculum link:

**Count up and down in hundredths**; recognise that hundredths arise when dividing an object by one hundred and dividing tenths by ten.

## Year 4 pupils should already know that:

- The denominator determines the number of equal parts the whole is divided into and the numerator shows how many of these equal parts are represented by the fraction, e.g. $\frac{1}{5}$, $\frac{2}{5}$, $\frac{3}{5}$, etc.
- When a shape or a group of objects is divided by 10 it results in ten equal parts
- We use division to help us with work with fractions

## Supporting understanding

Hundredths arise when dividing an object or quantity into a hundred equal parts.

It is useful to explore a range of familiar images that show hundredths.

**Dienes (Base 10) equipment**

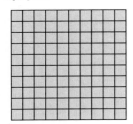

| 1 | 2 | 3 | 4 | 5 | 6 | 7 | 8 | 9 | 10 |
|---|---|---|---|---|---|---|---|---|----|
| 11 | 12 | 13 | 14 | 15 | 16 | 17 | 18 | 19 | 20 |
| 21 | 22 | 23 | 24 | 25 | 26 | 27 | 28 | 29 | 30 |
| 31 | 32 | 33 | 34 | 35 | 36 | 37 | 38 | 39 | 40 |
| 41 | 42 | 43 | 44 | 45 | 46 | 47 | 48 | 49 | 50 |
| 51 | 52 | 53 | 54 | 55 | 56 | 57 | 58 | 59 | 60 |
| 61 | 62 | 63 | 64 | 65 | 66 | 67 | 68 | 69 | 70 |
| 71 | 72 | 73 | 74 | 75 | 76 | 77 | 78 | 79 | 80 |
| 81 | 82 | 83 | 84 | 85 | 86 | 87 | 88 | 89 | 90 |
| 91 | 92 | 93 | 94 | 95 | 96 | 97 | 98 | 99 | 100 |

A metre stick also has 100 equal parts. Each centimetre is $\frac{1}{100}$ of a metre.

## Relationship between tenths and hundredths

Knowing the relationship between tenths and hundredths is imperative as it will later support comparing and calculating with decimals that do not share the same number of decimal places.

Knowing that $\frac{2}{10}$ or 0.2 is equal to $\frac{20}{100}$ or 0.20 will help when comparing it with the decimal 0.25 or $\frac{25}{100}$.

## In the classroom

Revisit the key point that the denominator determines the number of equal parts the whole is divided into.

*What do we know about the fractions with these denominators?*

$$\frac{1}{4} \quad \frac{1}{8} \quad \frac{1}{10} \quad \frac{1}{100}$$

Consider an image showing hundredths, e.g. a Dienes (base 10) hundred piece and a larger visual of a similar image.

Establish that each part is $\frac{1}{100}$ as it takes 100 of them to complete the whole. It has been divided into 100 equal parts.

*In the same way that we have counted in other fraction steps, we can also count in hundredths.*

Using the visual, count and label the hundredths. Pose these, or similar, questions for different groups to consider:

- *How many hundredths have we counted? How can we write this as a fraction?*

- *I am on $\frac{8}{100}$ and count on 3 hundredths. Where do I land?*

  Record as:

  $$\frac{8}{100} \cap \cap \cap \frac{11}{100}$$

- *What do you notice about $\frac{10}{100}$? Can we write this fraction in another way?*

- *How many more hundredths must we count to complete the whole? Can you explain why number bonds may be useful?*

Contextualise the concept by linking to the metre stick.

*This also has 100 equal parts.*

Discuss what each of these parts is called (centimetre) and how many are in the metre. *The prefix 'centi-' means 'hundredth'.*

Establish that 1 cm is $\frac{1}{100}$ of a metre and 10 cm is $\frac{10}{100}$ of a metre, which is equivalent to $\frac{1}{10}$ of a metre.

*This is also called a 'decimetre'.*

**ANSWERS**

Children's own working for all tasks

**Task C: Challenge:** Record in metres and centimetres, e.g. 1 m 12 cm or $1\frac{12}{100}$ m

# Task A (Independent task)

You will need a dice, counter and ten different 'hundredths' fraction cards.

1) Fill in the missing fractions on the image.
2) Take a fraction card and place your counter on this fraction.
3) Roll the dice.
4) Count on this many hundredths.
5) Record what you have done, e.g: $\frac{8}{100} \frown\frown\frown \frac{11}{100}$
6) Take a new fraction card and repeat.

| $\frac{91}{100}$ | $\frac{92}{100}$ | $\frac{93}{100}$ | $\frac{94}{100}$ | $\frac{95}{100}$ | $\frac{96}{100}$ | $\frac{97}{100}$ | $\frac{98}{100}$ | $\frac{99}{100}$ | $\frac{100}{100}$ |
|---|---|---|---|---|---|---|---|---|---|
| $\frac{81}{100}$ | $\frac{82}{100}$ | $\frac{83}{100}$ | $\frac{84}{100}$ | $\frac{85}{100}$ | $\frac{86}{100}$ | $\frac{87}{100}$ | $\frac{88}{100}$ | $\frac{89}{100}$ | $\frac{90}{100}$ |
| $\frac{71}{100}$ | $\frac{72}{100}$ | $\frac{73}{100}$ | $\frac{74}{100}$ | $\frac{75}{100}$ | $\frac{76}{100}$ | $\frac{77}{100}$ | $\frac{78}{100}$ | $\frac{79}{100}$ | $\frac{80}{100}$ |
| $\frac{61}{100}$ | $\frac{62}{100}$ | $\frac{63}{100}$ | $\frac{64}{100}$ | $\frac{65}{100}$ | $\frac{66}{100}$ | $\frac{67}{100}$ | $\frac{68}{100}$ | $\frac{69}{100}$ | $\frac{70}{100}$ |
| $\frac{51}{100}$ | $\frac{52}{100}$ | $\frac{53}{100}$ | $\frac{54}{100}$ | $\frac{55}{100}$ | $\frac{56}{100}$ | $\frac{57}{100}$ | $\frac{58}{100}$ | $\frac{59}{100}$ | $\frac{60}{100}$ |
| $\frac{41}{100}$ | $\frac{42}{100}$ | $\frac{43}{100}$ | $\frac{44}{100}$ | $\frac{45}{100}$ | $\frac{46}{100}$ | $\frac{47}{100}$ | $\frac{48}{100}$ | $\frac{49}{100}$ | $\frac{50}{100}$ |
| $\frac{31}{100}$ | $\frac{32}{100}$ | $\frac{33}{100}$ | $\frac{34}{100}$ | $\frac{35}{100}$ | $\frac{36}{100}$ | $\frac{37}{100}$ | $\frac{38}{100}$ | $\frac{39}{100}$ | |
| $\frac{21}{100}$ | | $\frac{23}{100}$ | $\frac{24}{100}$ | $\frac{25}{100}$ | $\frac{26}{100}$ | $\frac{27}{100}$ | $\frac{28}{100}$ | $\frac{29}{100}$ | $\frac{30}{100}$ |
| $\frac{11}{100}$ | $\frac{12}{100}$ | $\frac{13}{100}$ | $\frac{14}{100}$ | $\frac{15}{100}$ | $\frac{16}{100}$ | $\frac{17}{100}$ | $\frac{18}{100}$ | $\frac{19}{100}$ | $\frac{20}{100}$ |
| $\frac{1}{100}$ | $\frac{2}{100}$ | $\frac{3}{100}$ | $\frac{4}{100}$ | | $\frac{6}{100}$ | $\frac{7}{100}$ | $\frac{8}{100}$ | $\frac{9}{100}$ | $\frac{10}{100}$ |

# Task B (Independent task)

You will need a dice, ten different 'hundredths' fraction cards and a metre stick.

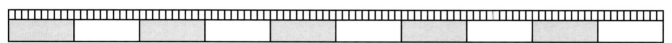

1) Label the metre stick, from 0, with $\frac{10}{100}$, $\frac{20}{100}$, up to $\frac{100}{100}$.
2) Take a fraction card and label it on the metre stick.
3) Roll the dice and count on or back this many hundredths of a metre.
4) Record what you have done, e.g:
$\frac{8}{100}$ m $\frown\frown\frown \frac{11}{100}$ m

5) Take a new fraction card and repeat.

**Challenge:**
1) What is the largest fraction that you have landed on?
2) How many centimetres is this fraction of a metre?

# Task C (Independent task)

You will need two dice and a metre stick.

1) Choose a hundredths fraction that is equivalent to a tenths fraction.
2) Label this on the metre stick.
3) Roll the two dice.
4) Choose one dice to be the step size, e.g. $\frac{3}{100}$ m, and the other to be the number of steps to take, e.g. 4 steps.

5) Record your steps, e.g. $\frac{20}{100}$ m, $\frac{23}{100}$ m, $\frac{26}{100}$ m, $\frac{29}{100}$ m, $\frac{32}{100}$ m.
6) Label your last step on your fraction bar, e.g. $\frac{32}{100}$ m.
7) How many centimetres is this fraction of a metre?
8) Choose a different tenths fraction and roll again.

**Challenge:** Try to go past the end of the fraction bar. How will you record your answers now?

# Understanding hundredths related to tenths

**UNIT 3**

## National Curriculum link:

Count up and down in hundredths; **recognise that hundredths arise when dividing an object by one hundred and dividing tenths by ten.**

## Year 4 pupils should already know that:

- When a shape or a group of objects is divided by 10 it results in ten equal parts
- When a shape or a group of objects is divided by 100 it results in one hundred equal parts
- We use division to help us work with fractions

## Supporting understanding

Tenths can be found by dividing an object or quantity into ten equal parts. Using knowledge of division, we know that, dividing each part by 10 again, we end up with one hundred equal parts.

Linking this idea to money can help to secure understanding.

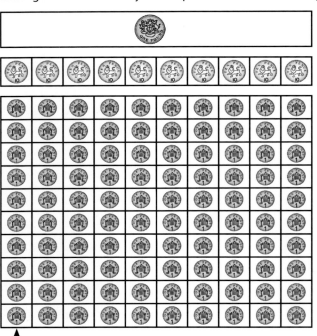

Each tenth of a pound (10p) is divided by 10, resulting in one hundred equal parts. Each hundredth is worth one pence (1p).

## Relationship between tenths and hundredths

The fraction bar can be used to explore how each tenth is divided by 10 to produce hundredths. Children can predict the number of hundredths equivalent to the number of tenths using knowledge of counting in tens and multiplication facts, e.g. 4 tenths is equal to 40 hundredths as $4 \times 10$ is 40.

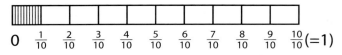

$0 \quad \frac{1}{10} \quad \frac{2}{10} \quad \frac{3}{10} \quad \frac{4}{10} \quad \frac{5}{10} \quad \frac{6}{10} \quad \frac{7}{10} \quad \frac{8}{10} \quad \frac{9}{10} \quad \frac{10}{10} (=1)$

## In the classroom

Using a tenths fraction bar (left), revisit the key point that when a shape or a group of objects is divided by 10 it results in ten equal parts.

Agree that each part is $\frac{1}{10}$ as it takes ten of them to complete the whole.

Pose the question: '*What if each of these ten parts is divided by 10 again?*'

Encourage children to visualise what would happen to the first tenth on our bar. Model dividing it into 10.

Pose the question: '*How many of these smaller parts will I have in total after we divide the second* (then third and fourth) *tenth by 10?*'

Establish that there are one hundred equal parts after all of the tenths have been divided by 10. Each of these parts is $\frac{1}{100}$ as it takes 100 of them to complete the whole.

Reinforce the objective: hundredths arise when dividing the whole by 100 or by dividing each tenth by 10.

Contextualise the concept by linking to money and developing the construction of the image (left).

Pose these, or similar, questions for different groups to consider:

- *How many 1 pence pieces are in £1?*
- *What fraction of a pound is 1p? How do you know?*
- *What fraction of a pound is 10p? How many hundredths is this?*

**ANSWERS**

**Task B: 1)** 1p **2)** 30p **3)** 10p **4)** 10 **5)** 3 **6)** 5 **7)** $\frac{1}{10}$ or $\frac{10}{100}$ which is 10p

**Task C: 1)** 3p **2)** 80p **3)** 15p **4)** 30 **5)** 6 **6)** 10 **7)** She gives Ishmal 16p, 17p, 18p or 19p, which is $\frac{16}{100}$, $\frac{17}{100}$, $\frac{18}{100}$ or $\frac{19}{100}$ of a pound; she could have 24p, 23p, 22p or 21p left (in order as above), which is $\frac{24}{100}$, $\frac{23}{100}$, $\frac{22}{100}$ or $\frac{21}{100}$ of a pound

## Task **A** (Guided learning with an adult)

| £1 |
|---|

| | | | | | | | | | |
|---|---|---|---|---|---|---|---|---|---|

Count in 10 pences up to £1. Agree that there are ten 10 pence coins in £1.

Use 10p coins and fraction bars to reinforce that each 10 pence is worth $\frac{1}{10}$ of a pound as there are ten equal parts.

**Challenge:**

Record the value of $\frac{2}{10}$ or $\frac{3}{10}$ of a pound, in pence.

Exchange 10p coins for the equivalent number of 1p coins.

Count sets of ten 1p coins as you go, to agree that one hundred 1p coins are equal to £1, so each 1 pence is $\frac{1}{100}$ of a pound as there are 100 equal parts.

## Task **B** (Independent task)

Copy and compete the following:

**1)** $\frac{1}{100}$ of £1 = ___ p

**2)** $\frac{3}{10}$ of £1 = ___ p

**3)** $\frac{10}{100}$ of £1 = ___ p

**4)** There are ___ hundredths in $\frac{1}{10}$

**5)** There are $\frac{30}{100}$ in ___ tenths

**6)** $\frac{}{10} = \frac{50}{100}$

**7)** Jamie has $\frac{2}{10}$ of a pound in his pocket. He gives Izzy $\frac{10}{100}$ of a pound.

What fraction of a pound does he have left? Can you show this in tenths and in hundredths?

How many pence is this?

## Task **C** (Independent task)

Copy and compete the following:

**1)** $\frac{3}{100}$ of £1 = ___ p

**2)** $\frac{8}{10}$ of £1 = ___ p

**3)** $\frac{15}{100}$ of £1 = ___ p

**4)** There are ___ hundredths in $\frac{3}{10}$

**5)** There are $\frac{60}{100}$ in ___ tenths

**6)** $\frac{}{10} = \frac{100}{100}$

**7)** Abi has $\frac{4}{10}$ of a pound in her pocket. She gives Ishmal more than $\frac{15}{100}$ of a pound but less than $\frac{2}{10}$.

How much could Abi have left in her pocket?

Show your answers in fractions and in pence.

# UNIT 4 Dividing one-digit numbers by 10 and 100

## National Curriculum link:

**Find the effect of dividing a one-** or two-**digit number by 10 and 100, identifying the value of the digits in the answer as ones, tenths and hundredths.**

## Year 4 pupils should already know that:

• When a shape or a group of objects is divided by 10 it results in ten equal parts
• When a shape or a group of objects is divided by 100 it results in one hundred equal parts
• Hundredths arise by dividing the whole by 100 or by dividing each tenth by 10
• Dividing by 10 makes a whole number 10 times smaller, e.g. $60 \div 10 = 6$

## Supporting understanding

In previous units, children have explored how tenths arise from dividing objects into ten equal parts and dividing quantities by ten. This unit will focus on using place value to secure understanding of tenths and hundredths.

In Year 3, children build on knowledge of place value and multiplication and division facts of 10 to explore dividing a one-digit number by 10.

| Units or ones • | tenths | |
|---|---|---|
| 1 | | |
| | 1 | $1 \div 10$ |
| 1 | | $\frac{1}{10} \times 10$ |

Fractions relate directly to division. This means that a familiar division sentence such as $20 \div 10$ can be written using fraction notation: $\frac{20}{10}$.

In the same way, $1 \div 10$ can be written as $\frac{1}{10}$ and $2 \div 10$ as $\frac{2}{10}$.

## Dividing a one-digit number by one hundred

A similar place value grid can be used to explore dividing one-digit numbers by 10 and 100.

| Units or ones • | tenths | hundredths | |
|---|---|---|---|
| 1 | | | |
| | 1 | | $1 \div 10$ |
| | | 1 | $1 \div 100$ or $\frac{1}{10} \div 10$ |

$1 \div 100$ can be written as $\frac{1}{100}$. This also shows that hundredths arise when tenths are divided by 10.

**ANSWERS**
**Task A: Challenge:** $4 \div 100 = \frac{4}{100}$
**Task B: Challenge:** Sami has made a mistake because he should have moved the 7 two places to the right, not just one; his answer should be $\frac{7}{100}$
**Task C:** E.g. for 2 hundredths, $2 \div 100$ or $\frac{2}{10} \div 10$, etc. **Challenge:** 2 in the tenths column and 4 in the hundredths column; as a decimal 0.24 (assessment opportunity)

## In the classroom

Revisit the key point that dividing by 10 makes a whole number 10 times smaller.

Invite children to write down a division fact of their choice that shows a whole number made 10 times smaller, e.g. $60 \div 10$ or $240 \div 10$.

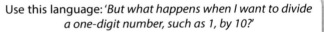

Use this language: 'But what happens when I want to divide a one-digit number, such as 1, by 10?'

Ask children to discuss and then model on a place value grid, making clear the number of places and direction that the digits must move.

Revisit the key point that when a shape or a group of objects is divided by 10 it results in ten equal parts.

So $1 \div 10$ results in ten equal parts or groups of $\frac{1}{10}$.

Record in a number sentence as $1 \div 10 = \frac{1}{10}$.

Look at $2 \div 10$ in the same way, as ten equal parts or groups of $\frac{2}{10}$.

Pose these, or similar, questions for different groups to consider:

• *What can you tell me about the size of the ten equal groups when I divide 3 by 10?*

• *And 6 by 10?*

• *What about 25 by 10?*

Ask children to record calculations in a number sentence as e.g. $6 \div 10 = \frac{6}{10}$.

Pose the problem that the calculation you now need to solve is not $1 \div 10$ but $1 \div 100$.

Ask children to discuss what they know about dividing by 10 and what we might need to do to divide by 100. Revisit the key point that hundredths arise when dividing the whole by 100 or by dividing each tenth by 10.

Model on a place value grid, making clear the number of places and direction that the digits must move.

# Task A (Independent task)

| Units or ones • | tenths |
|---|---|
|  |  |

- Take a digit card and put it on the place value grid.
- Divide the number by 10. Remember that you will need to move the digit card!
- Record in a number sentence using the ÷ symbol.
- Repeat with other digit cards.

**Challenge:**

Put the digit card 4 on the place value grid and then divide it by 100.

Record your new number sentence.

Say or write what was different this time.

# Task B (Independent task)

| Units or ones • | tenths | hundredths |
|---|---|---|
|  |  |  |

- Take a digit card and put it on the place value grid.
- Divide the number by 10. Remember that you will need to move the digit card!
- Record in a number sentence using the ÷ symbol.
- Now find out what happens when the number is divided by 100.
- Repeat with other digit cards.

**Challenge:**

Sami wrote $7 \div 100 = \frac{7}{10}$.

How do you know that he has made a mistake? Use this language: 'Sami has made a mistake because ___ .'

# Task C (Independent task)

You will need 'hundredths' cards, e.g. | 2 hundredths |

- Take a 'hundredth' card and write it as a fraction.
- Write two different division facts that were used to create your fraction.
- Check using a place value grid.
- Repeat with other fraction cards.

**HINT:** Think about how tenths can be divided to create hundredths.

**Challenge:**

Peter was playing a different game. He wrote this division fact: $24 \div 100 = \frac{24}{100}$.

What would this look like on the place value grid? Draw it.

Do you know how you would write this as a decimal?

# UNIT 5

# Dividing two-digit numbers by 10 and 100

## National Curriculum link:

**Find the effect of dividing a** one- or **two-digit number by 10 and 100, identifying the value of the digits in the answer as ones, tenths and hundredths.**

## Year 4 pupils should already know that:

- When a shape or a group of objects is divided by 10 it results in ten equal parts
- When a shape or a group of objects is divided by 100 it results in one hundred equal parts
- Hundredths arise when dividing the whole by 100 or by dividing each tenth by 10
- One tenth $\left(\frac{1}{10}\right)$ is equivalent to ten hundredths $\left(\frac{10}{100}\right)$

## Supporting understanding

In Unit 4, children divided one-digit numbers by 10 and then 100. They also considered the effect of dividing a number by 10 and 10 again. This links to work in previous units.

Here, the metre stick is divided into ten equal parts of 10 cm, where each part is worth $\frac{1}{10}$ of a metre. This is also known as a decimetre.

Each tenth is then divided into ten equal parts of 1 cm. Each part represents $\frac{1}{100}$ of the whole metre.

In this unit, children work with two-digit numbers and explore the effect of dividing by 10 and 100.

## Dividing a two-digit number by 10 and 100

The place value grid can be used to explore dividing 2-digit whole numbers by 10 and 100.

| Tens | Units or ones ● | tenths | hundredths | |
|------|------|------|------|------|
| 1 | 2 | | | |
| | 1 | 2 | | 12 ÷ 10 |
| | | 1 | 2 | 12 ÷ 100 |

12 ÷ 10 can be written as $1\frac{2}{10}$, whereas 12 ÷ 100 can be written as $\frac{12}{100}$ or $\frac{1}{10}$ and $\frac{2}{100}$. This can also be recorded as $\frac{1}{10} + \frac{2}{100}$.

It is also true that $12 ÷ 10 = \frac{12}{10}$, which is key learning for later on.

### ANSWERS

**Task A:** 4, $\frac{4}{10}$, 5, $\frac{5}{10}$, $1\frac{5}{10}$, $\frac{15}{100}$  **Challenge:** 6 ÷ 100 or $\frac{6}{10}$ ÷ 10

**Task B: 1)** $\frac{40}{100}$ or $\frac{4}{10}$ **2)** $4\frac{1}{10}$ **3)** $\frac{41}{100}$ **4)** 100 **5)** 23 **6)** 57 **7)** 60 ÷ 100

**8)** 35 ÷ 10 = $3\frac{5}{10}$ or 25 ÷ 10 = $2\frac{5}{10}$ or 15 ÷ 10 = $1\frac{5}{10}$

**Task C: 1)** $4\frac{5}{10}$ **2)** $\frac{45}{100}$ and 0.45 **3)** 29 ÷ 100 = $\frac{2}{10}$ and $\frac{9}{100}$, $\frac{29}{100}$

**4)** 65 **5)** 5 ÷ 10 = $\frac{5}{10}$ or 50 ÷ 100 = $\frac{50}{100}$ or $\frac{5}{10}$ **6)** 35 ÷ 100 = $\frac{35}{100}$ or $\frac{3}{10}$ and $\frac{5}{100}$, 77 ÷ 100 = $\frac{77}{100}$ or $\frac{7}{10}$ and $\frac{7}{100}$ and 91 ÷ 100 = $\frac{91}{100}$ or $\frac{9}{10}$ and $\frac{1}{100}$ **7)** Children's own clues

## In the classroom

Revisit the result of dividing one-digit numbers by 10 and 100 to reinforce the number of places and direction that the digits must move for each.

Use this language: *What happened to the one-digit whole number each time to result in these fractions: $\frac{2}{10}$ $\frac{1}{100}$ $\frac{5}{100}$?*

*What is different about this fraction: $\frac{10}{100}$?*

*What division calculation was used to create it?*

*Could it have been created as a result of dividing by 10?*

Ask children to discuss and then model on a place value grid, making clear the number of places and direction that the digits must move.

Look carefully at the positions of the digits.

*Why is the digit 1 in the tenths position and not in the hundredths?*

Revisit the key point that $\frac{10}{100}$ is equivalent to $\frac{1}{10}$.

Pose these, or similar, questions for different groups to consider:

- *What can you tell me about the size of the equal groups when I divide 30 by 10?*
- *And 30 divided by 100?*
- *What about 31 divided by 10 and by 100?*

Ask children to record calculations in a number sentence as e.g. 30 ÷ 100 = $\frac{30}{100}$.

Look at the position of the digit 3 on the place value grid. Reinforce that it is in the tenths position, as $\frac{30}{100}$ are equivalent to $\frac{3}{10}$.

Look in more detail at 31 ÷ 10 and 31 ÷ 100.

Model on the place value grid and establish the value of each digit before and after the division.

Use notation $3\frac{1}{10}$ and $\frac{31}{100}$. (Also consider, if appropriate, how $\frac{31}{100}$ can be written as $\frac{3}{10} + \frac{1}{100}$ because $\frac{10}{100}$ are equivalent to $\frac{1}{10}$.)

# Task **A** (Independent task or guided learning with an adult)

| Tens | Units or ones | tenths | hundredths |
|------|---------------|--------|------------|
| **4** | **0** | | |

$40 \div 10 =$ ____
$40 \div 100 =$ ____
$50 \div 10 =$ ____
$50 \div 100 =$ ____
$15 \div 10 =$ ____
$15 \div 100 =$ ____

- Use digit cards to make the number to be divided.
- Put the cards in the right place on a copy of the grid.
- Move the cards to complete the calculation.
- Write your calculation and the answer.

**Challenge:**

Jade put her digit cards on the place value grid.

She moved the cards to complete the calculation. Her answer was $\frac{6}{100}$.

What calculation did she do?

# Task **B** (Independent task)

**HINT:** There is more than one solution for question 8.

Copy and complete the following. Remember to use a place value grid to help you.

**1)** $40 \div 100 =$ ____

**2)** $41 \div 10 =$ ____

**3)** $41 \div 100 =$ ____

**4)** $16 \div$ ____ $= \frac{16}{100}$

**5)** ____ $\div 10 = 2\frac{3}{10}$

**6)** ____ $\div 100 = \frac{57}{100}$

In questions 7 and 8, use the clues to work out the division sentences that each child used.

**7)** The fraction that Sami made is equivalent to $\frac{6}{10}$ but he did not divide by 10.

**8)** Ami starts with a two-digit multiple of 5. She divides by 10. Her answer is less than 4 and is not a whole number. What fraction did she make and which division calculation did she use?

# Task **C** (Independent task)

Copy and complete the following. Remember to use a place value grid to help you.

**1)** $45 \div 10 =$ ____

**2)** $45 \div 100 =$ ____   Write this as a decimal.

**3)** $29 \div$ ____ $= \frac{2}{10}$ and $\frac{9}{100}$ or $\frac{29}{?}$

**4)** ____ $\div 10 = 6\frac{1}{2}$

**5)** The fraction that Paula made sits on the number line exactly halfway between 0 and 1.

She made this fraction by dividing by 10. She also made the same fraction by dividing by 100.

What fraction did she make and which two division calculations did she use?

**6)** Ishmal starts with a two-digit multiple of 7. He divides by 100. His answer has an odd number of tenths but also has an odd number of hundredths.

What fraction did he make and which division calculation did he use?

**7)** Now make up a clue of your own for a friend or your teacher to solve.

# UNIT 6
# Decimal representations of tenths and hundredths

## National Curriculum link:

**Recognise and write decimal equivalents of any number of tenths or hundredths.**

## Year 4 pupils should already know that:

- Decimals and fractions are different ways of expressing numbers and proportions
- There is an infinite range of numbers between two whole numbers on a number line
- There is a clear link between division and fractional representations
- The position of the digits in a decimal number show the value of each digit, just as they do for whole numbers

## Supporting understanding

A blank 100 square or base 10 equipment are powerful images that support understanding of decimals.

The shaded strip is worth $\frac{1}{10}$ of the whole as it takes ten of these to make up the whole.

Similarly, each of the shaded squares is worth $\frac{1}{100}$ of the whole as it takes one hundred of these to make up the whole.

This visual also makes it easy to see that $\frac{1}{10}$ is equivalent to $\frac{10}{100}$.

However, we are still using fraction notation, so what about decimals?

## Converting tenths and hundredths to decimals

A fraction can easily be converted to a decimal using division, e.g. $\frac{1}{10}$ can be converted using $1 \div 10$. This is the same division sentence that is used to create fractions in Units 4 and 5.

Converting fractions in this way can be explored on a calculator or by using the place value grid below, showing decimal representations.

| Units or ones • | tenths | hundredths | |
|---|---|---|---|
| 1 | | | |
| 0 | 1 | | $1 \div 10$ |
| 0 | 0 | 1 | $1 \div 100$ |

Zero is used as a place holder so that the values of the other digits are known.

**ANSWERS**
**Task B:** $\frac{5}{100}$, $\frac{2}{10}$, 0.4, $\frac{5}{10}$, $\frac{60}{100}$, 0.7
**Task C:** 0.3 and $\frac{3}{10}$, 0.6 and $\frac{6}{10}$, 0.9 and $\frac{9}{10}$, 0.75 and $\frac{75}{100}$, 0.85 and $\frac{85}{100}$, 0.09 and $\frac{9}{100}$ **Challenge:** Can cut 0.3 m and 0.6 m from two 1 metre lengths; a third length is needed for 0.9 m and the fourth for 0.75 m

## In the classroom

Revisit the key point that decimals and fractions are different ways of expressing numbers and proportions.

Introduce the 100 square or base 10 equipment.

Establish that each of the shaded strips (or 10 sticks) is worth $\frac{1}{10}$ of the whole as it takes ten of these pieces to make up the whole.

We can count in tenths until we have made up a whole $\frac{10}{10}$ (one tenth, two tenths, etc.). Label each strip.

Revisit the key point that there is a clear link between division and fractional representations.

Look at the symbol for division and a fractional representation, such as $\frac{1}{10}$. What similarities do children notice? How can $\frac{1}{10}$ be rewritten as a division calculation? ($1 \div 10$)

Ask children to use calculators to confirm the answer 0.1.

Ask children to quickly check $\frac{2}{10}$ and $\frac{3}{10}$ in the same way using the calculator.

Label the 100 square so it shows fraction and decimal equivalents.

*As mathematicians it is important that we can prove our findings in different ways.*

*How could we prove that $\frac{2}{10}$ is equal to 0.2 on the place value grid using the calculation $2 \div 10$? (2 moves one place to the right.)*

*How would this help us to find the decimal equivalent for $\frac{1}{100}$ or $\frac{2}{100}$? (The unit digit moves two places to the right.)*

# Task A (Guided learning with an adult)

Investigate the blank 100 square and base 10 equipment to ensure that children have a clear understanding of the way tenths relate to the whole.

| Tens | Units or ones • | tenths | hundredths |
|------|------------------|--------|------------|
|      |                  |        |            |

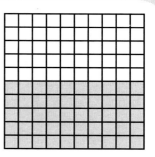

Show images of different fractions represented on 100 squares (see examples) for children to recreate using base 10 equipment, counting in tenths and recording the fraction shown. Include questions such as:

*How many tenths have we counted? How many more tenths would we need to count to make up the whole?*

Show where $\frac{3}{10}$ would be on a place value grid, with a zero denoting that there are no ones.

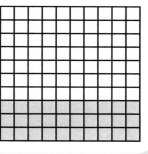

# Task B (Independent task)

| $\frac{5}{10}$ | $\frac{5}{100}$ | $\frac{2}{10}$ | 0.4 | $\frac{60}{100}$ | 0.7 | |

Use a place value grid or a calculator to help put these fraction and decimal cards in order.

Remember to explain your decisions.

> I know that ____ comes next because ____ .

**Challenge:** Write a decimal or fraction of your own and decide where it will go.

# Task C (Independent task)

Tom and Marie are making a kite. They are using 1 metre lengths of wood and ribbon and cutting them to the size they need.

Tom is very good at fractions but not so good with decimals. Luckily Marie is very good with decimals!

Help Tom and Marie check that their measurements are the same.

| Parts of kite | Marie's measurements | Tom's measurements |
|---------------|----------------------|---------------------|
| Wooden pieces 1 and 3 | 0.3 m | |
| Wooden pieces 3 and 4 | | $\frac{6}{10}$ of a metre |
| Wooden piece 5 | 0.9 m | |
| Wooden piece 6 | | $\frac{75}{100}$ of a metre |
| Ribbon | 0.85 m | |
| Bow | 0.09 m | |

**Challenge:** How can you show whether it is possible for Tom and Marie to use only four 1 metre lengths of wood for their kite?

# UNIT 7  Equivalent fractions of unit fractions

## National Curriculum link:
**Recognise and show, using diagrams, families of common equivalent fractions.**

## Year 4 pupils should already know that:
- Fractions can be represented by a range of images
- All fractions can be placed on the number line and some will sit in the same place as others
- Some fractions have the same value but do not look the same, e.g. $\frac{1}{2}$ and $\frac{5}{10}$

## Supporting understanding

In Key Stage 1, children will have met the equivalent fractions $\frac{1}{2}$ and $\frac{2}{4}$ through a range of images.
Circular fraction images will also have supported understanding of a half hour and a quarter of an hour, and that $\frac{1}{2}$ hour = $\frac{2}{4}$ hour.

Language structures can also be used to secure the concept of equivalence.

> I know these fractions are equivalent because they have the same value.

> $\frac{2}{4}$ is equivalent to $\frac{1}{2}$ because they are both worth the same fraction of a whole.

## Developing equivalence

Using fraction bars of the same length together provides a useful image showing which fractions are equivalent.

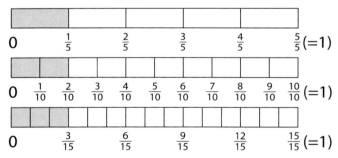

The images clearly show that $\frac{1}{5} = \frac{2}{10} = \frac{3}{15}$ and $\frac{2}{5} = \frac{4}{10} = \frac{6}{15}$, etc.

Therefore these groups of fractions will also have the same position on the number line.

## In the classroom

Use a range of images (including fraction bars) where $\frac{1}{3}$, $\frac{1}{4}$ and $\frac{1}{5}$ are shown in different ways, e.g.

Ask different groups to search for sets of equivalent fractions and practise using the language structures.

Return to the fraction $\frac{1}{5}$ and agree the other fraction images that have the same value, e.g. $\frac{2}{10}$, $\frac{3}{15}$, $\frac{4}{20}$.

Pose these, or similar, questions for different groups to consider:

- *What do you notice about the relationship between the numerator and denominator? How many twos are in 10? How many threes are in 15?*
- *What do you think comes next in this sequence of equivalent fractions? Why?*

Establish the importance of multiplication and division facts. Each numerator is $\frac{1}{5}$ of the denominator and each denominator is 5 times larger than the numerator.

Also look in more detail at the denominators:   $\frac{1}{5}$, $\frac{2}{10}$, $\frac{3}{15}$, $\frac{4}{20}$.

*Why would a fraction with the denominator 36 not be in my string of equivalents for $\frac{1}{5}$?*

We will use this information and fraction bars to help us search for other sets of equivalent fractions.

# Task **A** (Independent task)

You will need a set of fraction bars.

$$\boxed{\dfrac{1}{3}}$$

1) Find the fraction bar that shows thirds.
   - Use other bars to find other fractions that are worth the same as $\frac{1}{3}$.
   - Write them down as $\frac{1}{3} = $ ___ .
   - Practise using the language each time.

> ___ is equivalent to $\frac{1}{3}$ because they are both worth the same fraction of a whole.

2) How can you describe the relationship between the numerator and denominator each time? Remember to think about multiplication facts.

3) What other fractions are equivalent to $\frac{1}{3}$? You will not have fraction bars for these.

# Task **B** (Independent task)

Abi used the relationship between the numerator and denominator to help her find fractions that are equivalent to $\frac{1}{6}$.

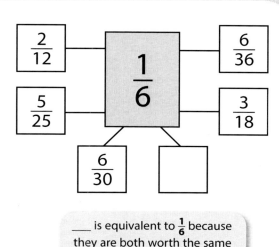

1) Check Abi's work and correct any mistakes she has made.

2) What is the relationship between the numerator and denominator for equivalent fractions of $\frac{1}{6}$?

3) Find some more equivalent fractions for the empty square. Prove you are correct using images or fraction bars.

4) Are the incorrect fractions equivalent to other fractions you know?

> ___ is equivalent to $\frac{1}{6}$ because they are both worth the same fraction of a whole.

# Task **C** (Independent task)

1) Use the relationship between the numerator and denominator to help find fractions that are equivalent.

2) What fraction is 4 of 48? And 6 of 72?

3) How can you use what you know about equivalent fractions for $\frac{1}{12}$ to help with equivalent fractions for $\frac{2}{12}$? Is there another equivalent fraction for $\frac{2}{12}$ with a numerator of 1?

> ___ is equivalent to $\frac{1}{12}$ because they are both worth the same fraction of a whole.

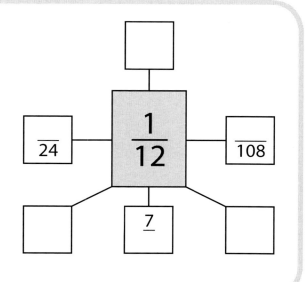

# UNIT 8  Equivalent non-unit fractions

## National Curriculum link:

Recognise and show, using diagrams, families of common equivalent fractions.

## Year 4 pupils should already know that:

- All fractions can be placed on the number line and some will sit in the same place as others
- Some fractions have the same value but do not look the same, e.g. $\frac{1}{5}$, $\frac{2}{10}$ and $\frac{3}{15}$

## Supporting understanding

In Year 3, children will have explored equivalents of fractions such as $\frac{3}{4}$, $\frac{2}{3}$ and $\frac{3}{5}$. All of these are already in their simplest form.

It is important that children recognise fraction bars that 'go together' and relate these to multiples, e.g. quarters and eighths, thirds and sixths, fifths and tenths.

They should be able to use the relevant language to explain that e.g. for every $\frac{1}{4}$ there are 2 lots of $\frac{1}{8}$, or $\frac{2}{8}$. This means that for $\frac{3}{4}$ there are three lots of $\frac{2}{8}$, or $\frac{6}{8}$.

## Developing equivalence of non-unit fractions

Children will need to recognise a range of images that show equivalent fractions and answer questions about them, e.g:

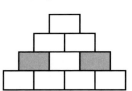

> What fraction does this image represent?

> How can I write this fraction in another way?

> How many more rectangles must I shade so that the image shows a fraction that is equivalent to $\frac{3}{5}$?

Again, using the language structure here alongside fraction bars will confirm that $\frac{6}{10}$ is equivalent to $\frac{3}{5}$.

> For every $\frac{1}{5}$ there are $\frac{2}{10}$ so $\frac{6}{10}$ is equivalent to $\frac{3}{5}$.

### ANSWERS

**Task A: 1)** $\frac{3}{9}$; $\frac{1}{3}$ **2)** 3; fraction bars (or similar) showing that $\frac{6}{9}$ is equivalent to $\frac{2}{3}$ **Challenge:** 4

**Task B: 1)** $\frac{2}{12}$; $\frac{1}{6}$ and fraction bars **2)** 6; fraction bars (or similar) showing that $\frac{8}{12}$ is equivalent to $\frac{4}{6}$ **3)** $\frac{2}{3}$

**Challenge:** $\frac{3}{18}$ and $\frac{9}{18}$

**Task C: 1)** $\frac{3}{24}$; $\frac{1}{8}$; $\frac{2}{16}$, etc. **2)** 12; $\frac{15}{24} = \frac{5}{8}$ proved with number line, fraction bars or other image **3)** 20 $\left(\frac{5}{6}\right)$ and 10 $\left(\frac{5}{12}\right)$

**Challenge:** 3 $\left(\frac{1}{8}\right)$, 9 $\left(\frac{3}{8}\right)$, 15 $\left(\frac{5}{8}\right)$, 21 $\left(\frac{7}{8}\right)$

## In the classroom

> Revisit fraction images that are equivalent to $\frac{1}{5}$ and ask children to describe the relationship between the numerator and denominator (as in Unit 7):
>
> $$\frac{1}{5} = \frac{2}{10} = \frac{3}{15} = \frac{4}{20} = \frac{5}{25}$$
>
> Establish any patterns: the denominators are all multiples of 5 and the numerators are going up in ones.

> Ask children to consider the question related to the image shown left:
>
> - *How many more rectangles must I shade so that the image shows a fraction that is equivalent to $\frac{3}{5}$?*

> Compare fraction bars for fifths and tenths to establish that $\frac{6}{10}$ is equivalent to $\frac{3}{5}$, because for every $\frac{1}{5}$ there are $\frac{2}{10}$.
> Use this language: *'For every $\frac{1}{5}$ there are $\frac{2}{10}$ so $\frac{6}{10}$ is equivalent to $\frac{3}{5}$.'*
> Create a list of other equivalents for $\frac{3}{5}$.
> *What patterns do you see this time?* (The denominators continue to be multiples of 5, but the numerators are now multiples of 3.)

> Model the transition of fraction bars to fractions on a number line. *We can now place equivalent fractions for $\frac{1}{5}$ and $\frac{3}{5}$ on the number line.*
>
> Pose these, or similar, questions for different groups to consider:
>
> - *Where should we place $\frac{1}{2}$ on the number line? How many tenths is this?*
>
> - *We know that $\frac{5}{25}$ is equivalent to $\frac{1}{5}$; how can we use this to find an equivalent for $\frac{4}{5}$?*
>
> - *We do not have an equivalent in fifths for any of the odd tenths. Why do you think this is? Can you suggest any equivalents we could use?* (Focus particularly on hundredths, but also consider twentieths to help to establish patterns.)

# Task A (Independent task or guided learning with an adult)

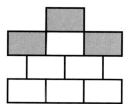

1) What fraction does the image represent?
   How can you write this fraction in another way?

2) How many more rectangles must I shade so that
   the image shows a fraction that is equivalent to $\frac{2}{3}$?
   Draw or use a fraction bar to prove that it has the same value as $\frac{2}{3}$.

**Challenge:**

Izzy also drew this fraction bar to show $\frac{2}{3}$. How many sixths are equivalent to $\frac{2}{3}$?

# Task B (Independent task or guided learning with an adult)

1) What fraction does this image represent?
   How can you write this fraction in another way?
   Draw the fraction bar that matches this fraction.

2) How many more squares must I shade so that the image
   shows a fraction that is equivalent to $\frac{4}{6}$? Draw or use a
   fraction bar to prove that it has the same value as $\frac{4}{6}$.

3) Can you write this fraction in another way?

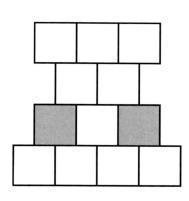

**Challenge:**

Pete used this language to help him with equivalent fractions.
What equivalent fractions is he describing?

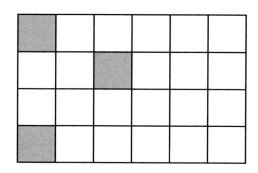

For every $\frac{1}{6}$ there are $\frac{3}{?}$ so $\frac{3}{6}$ is
equivalent to $\frac{9}{?}$.

# Task C (Independent task)

1) What fraction does this image represent?
   How can you write this fraction in another way?

2) How many more squares must I shade so that the image
   shows a fraction that is equivalent to $\frac{5}{8}$?
   Find a way to prove that it has the same value as $\frac{5}{8}$.

3) How many squares must be shaded to show $\frac{5}{6}$? And $\frac{5}{12}$?

**Challenge:**

Sami shaded an odd number of squares on the same image and wrote down the fraction it showed.
The fraction did not have 24 as the denominator.
How many squares did he shade? What fraction does this show? Try to find more than one solution.

# Other decimal equivalents

## National Curriculum link:

**Recognise and write decimal equivalents to $\frac{1}{4}$, $\frac{1}{2}$, $\frac{3}{4}$.**

## Year 4 pupils should already know that:

- Decimals and fractions are different ways of expressing numbers and proportions
- There is a clear link between division and both fractional and decimal representations
- The position of the digits in a decimal number shows the value of each digit

## Supporting understanding

In Unit 6, we looked at the relationship between each row, i.e. tenth, and the whole and each individual square, i.e. hundredth, and the whole.

As part of the lesson, children converted fractions as tenths and hundredths to decimals using the place value grid and a calculator. They found that $\frac{1}{10}$ = 0.1 and $\frac{1}{100}$ = 0.01, and so on.

The image shows $\frac{1}{2}$, but using what we already know, each row is worth $\frac{1}{10}$ so $\frac{1}{2}$ is equal to $\frac{5}{10}$ (or $\frac{50}{100}$).

However, we also know that each $\frac{1}{10}$ is 0.1 as a decimal and $\frac{5}{10}$ is 0.5. So $\frac{1}{2}$ as a decimal is 0.5.

We can also prove this to be true using a calculator and the division calculation 1 ÷ 2.

## Decimal equivalents of $\frac{1}{4}$ and $\frac{3}{4}$

Using a calculator and the division sentences 1 ÷ 4 and 3 ÷ 4 will confirm the decimal equivalents of $\frac{1}{4}$ and $\frac{3}{4}$.

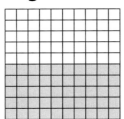

However, the 100 square again provides a powerful visual.

The image shows $\frac{1}{4}$, but is made up of $\frac{2}{10}$ (0.2) and $\frac{5}{100}$ (0.05), or $\frac{25}{100}$.

| Units or ones • | tenths | hundredths |
|:---:|:---:|:---:|
| 0 | 2 | 5 |

Similarly, $\frac{3}{4}$ is made up of $\frac{7}{10}$ and $\frac{5}{100}$ or $\frac{75}{100}$, i.e. 0.75.

### ANSWERS

**Task A:** In order: 0.25, 0.4, 0.5, 0.75, 0.9; 0.5 = $\frac{1}{2}$ **Challenge:** Three rows, which is larger than $\frac{1}{4}$

**Task B: 1)** 0.6 **2)** 0.3 **3)** 0.25 and 0.5 together as 0.75 **4)** 0.2

**Task C:** 0.1, 0.2, 0.3, **0.5, 0.75**, 0.8, etc; the answers in bold can have a range of solutions as long as the smaller of the two is 0.5 or more and the second is less than 0.8, and they must also have a difference of $\frac{1}{4}$ as stated, e.g. 0.51 and 0.76

## In the classroom

Revisit the 100 square image used in Unit 6.

Count the rows in steps of 0.1 and then the squares in steps of 0.01, making sure that the equivalence between 10 hundredths and 1 tenth is secure.

---

Show a range of different shaded 100 squares, e.g. $\frac{2}{10}$, $\frac{5}{10}$ and $\frac{7}{10}$. Ask children to describe them in tenths and then in decimals. (This could be done as a 'barrier' game where partners describe the unseen visual to their partner.)

---

Return to the image showing $\frac{5}{10}$.

*What other fraction equivalent to $\frac{5}{10}$ does this show?* $\left(\frac{1}{2}\right)$

*So, what do we now know about the decimal equivalent of $\frac{1}{2}$?*

Confirm this by showing $\frac{5}{10}$ on the place value grid.

---

Ask children to consider the fractions $\frac{1}{4}$ and $\frac{3}{4}$ in the same way, thinking about representing them in full rows and parts of a row.

Pose these, or similar, questions for different groups to consider:

- *How would you describe what $\frac{1}{4}$ looks like on a 100 square? How many full rows will there be? And what else?*

- *What do you know about the relationship between a quarter and a half? How does this help you to describe $\frac{1}{4}$ on the 100 square?*

- *How would you describe what $\frac{3}{4}$ looks like on the 100 square? How many tenths and how many hundredths is this? How much more than $\frac{1}{2}$ is it?*

---

Confirm by showing $\frac{1}{4}$ as $\frac{2}{10}$ and $\frac{5}{100}$ on the place value grid and $\frac{3}{4}$ as $\frac{7}{10}$ and $\frac{5}{100}$.

## Task A (Independent task or guided learning with an adult)

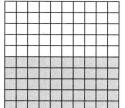 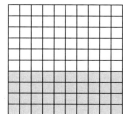 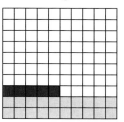 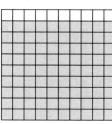 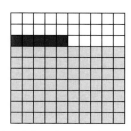

- Take each shaded 100 square and write down the number of tenths and hundredths that it shows.
- Use the place value grid to record the tenths and hundredths.
- Write the fraction as a decimal.
- Put all of your decimals in order from smallest to largest.
- Which of your decimals is equal to $\frac{1}{2}$?

**Challenge:**

What would the decimal 0.3 look like on the 100 square?

Describe the number of rows that will be shaded.

Is this larger or smaller than $\frac{1}{4}$?

| Units or ones • | tenths | hundredths |
|---|---|---|
|  |  |  |
|  |  |  |
|  |  |  |
|  |  |  |
|  |  |  |
|  |  |  |

## Task B (Independent task or guided learning with an adult)

Izzy and Tom each picked a decimal number from this place value grid and shaded it on the 100 square.

Use the clues to work out which decimals they picked each time.

**1)** Izzy shaded more than $\frac{1}{2}$ of the 100 square, but only used tenths.

**2)** Tom shaded a decimal that was only $\frac{5}{100}$ more than $\frac{1}{4}$ of his 100 square.

**3)** Izzy shaded two different decimals on the same 100 square, but it looked just like another decimal on the grid!

   What were they and what other decimal did they look like?

**4)** Tom shaded $\frac{1}{5}$ of the 100 square.

| Units or ones • | tenths | hundredths |
|---|---|---|
| 0 | 6 |  |
| 0 | 7 | 5 |
| 0 | 3 |  |
| 0 | 5 |  |
| 0 | 2 | 5 |
| 0 | 2 |  |

## Task C (Independent task)

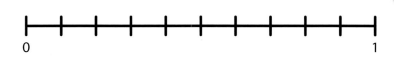

Ishmal picked six different decimal numbers and placed them on this number line.

Use the clues to find out which six decimal numbers he picked.

Write Ishmal's six numbers in the correct places on the number line.

Try to find more than one solution.

**CLUES:**
- Three of the numbers are less than $\frac{1}{2}$.
- One of the numbers is equivalent to $\frac{1}{5}$.
- The largest number is 0.05 more than $\frac{3}{4}$.
- The smallest number is 3 tenths less than $\frac{2}{5}$.
- One of the numbers is 0.05 more than $\frac{1}{4}$.
- The remaining two numbers have a difference of $\frac{1}{4}$.

# UNIT 10  Problems about fractions and decimals (1)

## National Curriculum link:

[Non-statutory guidance] **Practise counting using simple fractions and decimals, both forwards** and backwards.

## Year 4 pupils should already know that:

- Decimals and fractions are different ways of expressing numbers and proportions
- All fractions can be shown as decimals using division to help us, e.g. $\frac{1}{2}$ as $1 \div 2 = 0.5$
- Knowing fraction and decimal equivalents is helpful, especially when solving problems

## Supporting understanding

In Unit 3, children explored fractions of money, building on an image of the whole pound and ten tenths of a pound, or ten 10p coins. Each tenth was then divided by 10 to create one hundred hundredths of a pound, or one hundred 1p coins.

By adapting the 100 square, we can now use the hundred 1p coins to represent a contextualised square, as used in previous units.

Each row is worth $\frac{1}{10}$ or $\frac{10}{100}$ of a pound and can be shown as a decimal, as £0.10.

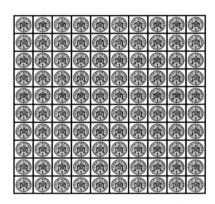

As there are 100 pence in a pound, we can use the fraction $\frac{10}{100}$ to help children understand that in money, the decimal 0.1 is shown with zero in the hundredths column, i.e. as £0.10.

## Solving problems with more than one solution

Children should be encouraged to look for more than one solution, and therefore must have access to a range of problems that require this.

As teachers, we should model making generalisations and show children how to organise their thinking and their results, and consider more than one solution.

### ANSWERS
**Task B: 1)** Sally 35p and Tom 35p; Sally $\frac{10}{100} + \frac{8}{100} = \frac{18}{100}$ (0.18), $\frac{18}{100} + \frac{7}{100} = \frac{25}{100}$ (0.25; takes 25p), then a further 10p with $\frac{6}{100}$ and $\frac{9}{100}$ or with $\frac{1}{100}$ and $\frac{4}{100}$; Tom $\frac{14}{100} + \frac{3}{100} = \frac{17}{100}$ (0.17), $\frac{17}{100} + \frac{8}{100} = \frac{25}{100}$ (0.25; takes 25p), then a further 10p with $\frac{4}{100}$ and $\frac{1}{100}$
**2)** E.g. Sally same as for question 1, but Tom 'missing' tenths and 0.25 (various solutions possible); solution to include Tom's number sentences
**Task C: 1)** Each 85p, e.g. Sally: $\frac{32}{100} + \frac{8}{100}$ (takes 10p), then $\frac{12}{100}$, $\frac{12}{100}$ and $\frac{11}{100}$ to land on $\frac{75}{100}$ (takes 75p); Tom: $\frac{34}{100} + \frac{6}{100}$ (takes 10p), then $\frac{12}{100}$, $\frac{12}{100}$ and $\frac{11}{100}$ to land on $\frac{75}{100}$ (takes 75p); solution to include dice rolled **2)** Nothing, by 'missing' tenths and 0.75 (various solutions possible); solution to include number sentences and dice rolled **3)** E.g. Sally same as for question 1, but Tom landing on $\frac{75}{100}$ and not landing on a tenth

## In the classroom

Practise counting in different fraction steps on a counting stick or number line. In unison, different groups should count in tenths, others in hundredths and the rest in decimal steps. This will help to secure equivalent values.

Stop the count at 0.4.
Pose these, or similar, questions for different groups to consider:
- *How many more tenths do I need to count to reach $\frac{1}{2}$?*
- *How many tenths do I need to count to reach 0.8?*
- *How many hundredths do I need to count to reach 0.8?*

Now consider decimal equivalents of $\frac{1}{4}$ and $\frac{3}{4}$ by posing the following questions:
- *Where would the decimals 0.25 and 0.75 be on the counting stick? Explain your thinking.*
- *What if the whole is now worth £1: what would these decimals be worth?*

It is harder to see all the hundredths in this image (left), so we can use another familiar image (100 square) to clearly show that each tenth (now arranged in rows) is equivalent to 10 hundredths.
Mask $\frac{1}{2}$ and then $\frac{1}{4}$ and $\frac{3}{4}$ of the pound to reinforce that the decimal equivalent of each is £0.50, £0.25 and £0.75, as each can be represented by the fractions $\frac{50}{100}$, $\frac{25}{100}$ and $\frac{75}{100}$.

Introduce the problem and game that will be developed during the lesson.

*Sally and Tom are playing 'Penny Swap'. They take it in turns to roll two dice to make hundredths.*

*10p can be collected by landing on a square that completes a tenth of a pound, 25p can be collected by landing on $\frac{25}{100}$ and 75p can be collected by landing on $\frac{75}{100}$. The player to reach the top row having collected the most money is the winner.*

*On her first turn, Sally lands on $\frac{8}{100}$. On her second turn she then rolls 2 and 5. She can choose to use either number, as $\frac{2}{100}$ or $\frac{5}{100}$ or their sum, $\frac{7}{100}$, and move her counter this number of places.*

*What should she do and why?*

*She records her move as $\frac{8}{100} + \frac{2}{100} = \frac{10}{100}$ (0.1) and takes 10p.*

# Task A (Independent task)

Play 'Penny Swap' with a partner on a 100 square with a 1p coin on each square.

- Take it in turns to roll two dice.
- Use the numbers to make hundredths, e.g. $\frac{3}{100}$ and $\frac{4}{100}$.
- Choose to use either number or the sum of them, e.g. $\frac{7}{100}$. Move your counter this number of places.
- Record the move you make in a number sentence.
- Remember to try to make tenths or land on $\frac{25}{100}$ or $\frac{75}{100}$.

# Task B (Guided learning with an adult)

Sally's counter is on $\frac{10}{100}$ and Tom's is on $\frac{14}{100}$.
These are the dice they rolled on their next four goes.

| Sally | | | | |
|---|---|---|---|---|
| Tom | | | | |

1) Investigate to find the most amount of money Sally and Tom could have each collected in these four goes.

   Record the number sentences each wrote down.

2) Now try to find a solution where Sally has collected the most money.

   Record Tom's number sentences this time.

# Task C (Independent task)

Sally's counter is on $\frac{32}{100}$ and Tom's is on $\frac{34}{100}$.
Investigate to find:

1) The greatest amount of money Sally and Tom could each collect in their next four goes.

   Record the dice they rolled and the number sentences they wrote.

2) The least amount of money Sally and Tom could each collect in their next four goes.

   Record the dice they rolled and the number sentences they wrote.

3) A solution where Sally collects 10p more than Tom.

**UNIT 11**

# Rounding decimals

## National Curriculum link:
**Round decimals with one decimal place to the nearest whole number.**

## Year 4 pupils should already know that:
- The position of the digits in a decimal number show the value of each digit
- It is important to know the position of numbers on the number line and the different boundaries they sit between

## Supporting understanding

When rounding whole numbers, children have first to be able to recognise the boundaries that a number sits between, e.g. to round 36 to the nearest 10 requires children to know what tens boundaries (multiples of 10) it sits between.

Children tend to be more secure with identifying the next multiple of 10 than finding the previous one, in this case mistaking it for 20 rather than 30.

Describing 36 as *30 and 6 more* or *6 more than 30* helps to overcome this barrier.

## Rounding decimals to the nearest whole number

We know that when rounding a number to the nearest ten, we look at the units digit and round up to the next ten when it has the value of 5 or more.

The same principle applies here, but this time when rounding decimals with one decimal place, e.g. 3.6, to the nearest whole number, we must look at the value of the tenths digit.

When the whole number boundaries are identified, we can round up or down accordingly.

Again, the language *3.6 is 3 and 0.6 more* or *0.6 more than 3* will help here.

**ANSWERS**
**Task A: 1–4)** Diagrams showing the multiples of 10 on either side of the numbers with 30, 30 and 40 underlined, respectively **5)** Children's explanations, perhaps with diagrams
**Task B: 1–5)** Diagrams showing whole numbers on either side with 7, 13, 10 and 20 underlined, respectively **6)** Diagram for 12.1, 12.2, 12.3 or 12.4 and question marks replaced accordingly
**Task C: 1)** Diagrams for 20.1, 20.2, 20.3 or 20.4 with question marks replaced accordingly **2)** Smallest 14.5 and largest 15.4, although some children may exceed expectations with, say, 15.49
**3)** 13 **4)** 7 **5)** 160 **6)** 5 **7)** First number rounding to 9, e.g. 9.1

## In the classroom

Revisit identifying the boundaries that numbers sit between. Ask children to identify the next and previous multiples of 10 for these numbers:
36  95  103  194  30

Use this language: *'30 and 6 more'* or *'6 more than 30'* to secure understanding and address any misconceptions.

*I want to make some estimates, so I need to round each of the numbers to the nearest ten. Why does rounding numbers help to make estimates?*

Establish that it is easier calculating with multiples of 10.

*So 103 + 36 as an estimate is 100 + 40 = 140.*

Ask children to discuss the rules for rounding to the nearest multiple of 10.

*Why does 36 not round down to 30? Why does 30 not round down to 20?*

Now change the numbers so that they are all 10 times smaller (divided by 10):
3.6  9.5  10.3  19.4  3

Pose these, or similar, questions for different groups to consider:

- *What is the same and what is different about this set of numbers?*

- *Which whole numbers do each of these sit between?*

- *I need to use rounding to help me make estimates again, but what should I do this time?*

Use a number line to establish where 3.6 sits and the value of the tenths digit. Count on and back to the next or previous whole number to confirm that 3.6 rounds to 4 in the same way that 36 rounds to 40.

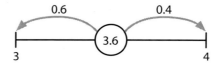

# Task A (Independent task)

Find the next and previous multiple of 10 for these numbers.
Record them in the way shown for 23.

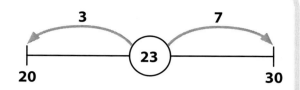

**1)** 27          **2)** 34          **3)** 41

**4)** Now use what you have found to help you round each number to the nearest 10.
Put a line under the multiple of 10 you choose.

**5)** Pete has to round 2.7, 3.4 and 4.1 to the nearest whole number.
How can you help him?

# Task B (Independent task)

Find the next and previous whole number for these numbers.
Record it in the way shown for 2.3.

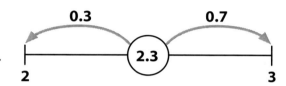

**1)** 6.7          **2)** 13.4          **3)** 9.5          **4)** 20.4

**5)** Now use what you have found to help you round each number to the nearest whole number.
Put a line under the whole number you choose.

**6)** Izzy drew this picture to help her round her number
to the nearest whole number. It rounded to 12.
What could her number have been?
Copy and complete Izzy's work.

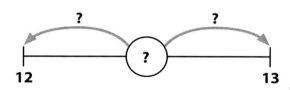

# Task C (Independent task or guided learning with an adult)

**1)** Tom drew this picture to help him round his number to
the nearest whole number. It rounded to 20.
What could his number have been? Copy and complete
Tom's work. Find more than one solution.

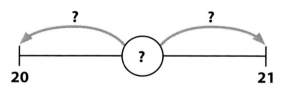

**2)** Jade rounded her number. It rounded to 15.
What could her number have been? What is the smallest and largest possible number?

Now use what you know about rounding to make some estimates for these calculations.

**3)** 9.7 + 3.1 estimate ____          **4)** 13.4 – 5.9 estimate ____

**5)** 16.2 × 10.1 estimate ____          **6)** 25 ÷ 4.7 estimate ____

**7)** ____ + 4.8 estimate 14, but what could the calculation be?

# UNIT 12  Comparing numbers with decimal places

## National Curriculum link:
Compare numbers with the same number of decimal places up to two decimal places.

## Year 4 pupils should already know that:
- The position of the digits in a decimal number shows the value of each digit
- One tenth is equivalent to 0.1 and one hundredth is equivalent to 0.01
- It is important to know the position of numbers on the number line and the different boundaries they sit between

## Supporting understanding

In previous units, the blank 100 square and the place value grid have been used to help secure understanding of tenths and hundredths and their decimal equivalents.

We can use the same images when comparing decimal numbers or develop the use of base 10 apparatus to make numbers.

Look at the different ways that we can represent 0.25:

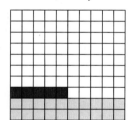 

$0.25 = \frac{2}{10} + \frac{5}{100}$ or $\frac{25}{100}$

| Units or ones | tenths | hundredths |
|---|---|---|
| 0 | 2 | 5 |

Each shows the value of the digit 2 and digit 5 within the number.

With the base 10 visual, the whole (100 flat piece) should be introduced so that the use of the apparatus for decimals is clear.

## Comparing decimals

Children who are unsure of the importance of zero as a place holder and its significance in different positions (that is, it is not significant in a number such as 0312 but significant in 3120) will need additional support to secure this vital concept.

Consider the numbers 1.02 and 1.20, where each includes a zero. The zero is not significant in 1.20 but will be useful later on when children compare numbers with a different number of decimal places. However, the zero in 1.02 is important as a place holder so the digit 2 sits in the hundredths position.

## In the classroom

Show several different images representing 0.25.

Revisit the key point that the position of the digits in a decimal number shows the value of each digit.

*We also know that one tenth is equivalent to 0.1 and one hundredth is equivalent to 0.01, so how many tenths and hundredths are in 0.25?*

Record this as $0.25 = \frac{2}{10} + \frac{5}{100}$ and also as $\frac{25}{100}$.

---

Ask children to record the place value of some of these numbers in the same way:

0.35   0.34   0.29   0.28   3.5   3.4   2.9   2.8

*What do you notice about some of the numbers?* (Same digits but different values; four numbers have only one digit after the decimal point.)

---

Start by comparing 3.5 and 3.4 and establish that they both have 3 units, but 3.4 has $\frac{1}{10}$ less than 3.5, or $\frac{10}{100}$ less.

Record as 3.4 < 3.5 and confirm using base 10 apparatus or the 100 square image.

Ask children to compare 2.9 and 2.8 in the same way or move on to compare e.g. 0.35 and 0.34. They should describe or use images or apparatus to prove which number is larger.

---

Establish that it is easier to compare numbers that have the same number of decimal places.

This is also the same for measurement, e.g. it is much easier to compare 1.25 litres with 1.35 litres.

### ANSWERS
**Task A: 1)** E.g. $2.6 = 2 + \frac{6}{10}$ **2)** As in example **3)** E.g. 2.2 < 2.6
**Challenge:** 1.3, 1.5, 2.2, 2.6, 5.4, 5.7
**Task B: 1)** E.g. 2.1, 0.3, 3.2, 0.1, 0.2 **2)** E.g. $2.1 = 2 + \frac{1}{10}$ **3)** E.g 0.3 <
2.1 **4)** E.g. 0.1, 0.2, 0.3, 2.1, 3.2 **5)** E.g. 0.12 $\left(\frac{1}{10} + \frac{2}{100}\right)$, 0.31 and 1.32
**Task C:** E.g. 2.13 < 2.14 with values shown, e.g. $2 + \frac{13}{100}$
**Challenge:** E.g. 0.54, 1.02 and 1.23 litres

# Task **A** (Independent task)

Here are three pairs of numbers:

| 2.6 | 2.2 | | 5.7 | 5.4 | | 1.3 | 1.5 |

1) Start with the first pair and show how much the digits in each number are worth, e.g. $1.6 = 1 + \frac{6}{10}$.
2) Make each number using base 10 apparatus, e.g. 1.2 is:
3) Now compare the two numbers using the symbol <.

Repeat for the other pairs.

**Challenge:** Can you write all six numbers in order? Put the smallest one first.

# Task **B** (Independent task)

1) Use the digit cards to make **five** different numbers showing units and tenths.
   You can use a card more than once.
2) Show how much the digits in each number are worth, e.g. $1.2 = 1 + \frac{2}{10}$.
3) Use the base 10 images to help you compare different pairs of numbers.
   Write what you find out using the < symbol.
4) Now write all five numbers in order. Put the smallest first.
5) Use the same set of digit cards to make three different capacities including hundredths, e.g. 0.23 litres. Show how much the digits in each number are worth and then order them.

| 0 | 1 |
| 2 | 3 |

# Task **C** (Independent task)

Sami uses these digit cards to make different decimal numbers.

☐ . ☐ ☐  <  ☐ . ☐ ☐

The ones value is the same in both numbers.
Help Sami find different ways to make this true.
Record the value of the digits each time, e.g. $1.23 = 1 + \frac{23}{100}$.

**Challenge:**

If each digit card is used only once, can Sami use all the cards to make three amounts in litres that will sit on this number line?

| 0 | 0 |
| 1 | 1 |
| 2 | 2 |
| 3 | 4 |
| 5 | |

0.5 litres ————————————— 1.3 litres

# Solving problems about measure with decimals to two decimal plac

## National Curriculum link:

**Solve simple measure and money problems involving fractions and decimals to two decimal places.**
[Non-statutory guidance] **Practise counting using simple fractions and decimals, both forwards and backward**

## Year 4 pupils should already know that:

- Decimals and fractions are different ways of expressing numbers and proportions
- There is an infinite range of numbers that sit between two whole numbers on a number line
- The positions of the digits in a decimal number show the value of each digit

## Supporting understanding

Counting on and back in decimal steps will help prepare children for calculating with decimals.

Place value charts support counting and secure understanding of the value of each digit, as children can see how each number is formed.

| ①   | 2    | 3    | 4    | 5     | 6    | 7    | 8    | 9    |
|------|------|------|------|-------|------|------|------|------|
| 0.1  | ⓪.2  | 0.3  | 0.4  | 0.5   | 0.6  | 0.7  | 0.8  | 0.9  |
| 0.01 | 0.02 | 0.03 | 0.04 | ⓪.05  | 0.06 | 0.07 | 0.08 | 0.09 |

The numbers circled are 1 one, 2 tenths and 5 hundredths, which combine to equal 1.25.

Decimal place value cards will also support here.

Children can explore what happens when we count on in tenths, i.e. hundredths remain the same, tenths increase by one each time and the ones increase once 10 tenths have been counted.

> 1
> 0.2
> 0.05

## Solving problems about decimal numbers

Children should have regular opportunities to make decisions about the position of decimals or fractions on a number line.

Consider the number strip and paper clip shown here and the following questions:

*When the start of the line is 0 and the end is 1 kg, what number could the clip represent?* (E.g. 0.25 kg.)

*When the start is still 0 but the end is 2 kg, why can't the clip represent the same number?*

*What could it represent now?* (E.g. 0.5 kg.)

*Where will 0.5 kg sit on the 0 to 4 kg number line?*

> I know ... so ....
> It could be ... because ....
> It couldn't be ... because ....

Language structures will continue to support children's reasoning and explanations.

## In the classroom

Use the place value chart, or similar, to count in different steps, e.g. start at 1 and count in steps of 0.2, paying particular attention to the step from 1.8 to 2.

Stop at 2.6. *How has this number been made?* (2 and 0.6)

Now continue the count in steps of 0.01, stopping at 2.75. *How has this number been made?*

Ask different groups to quickly find the parts that will be needed for 3.5, then 3.25, then 3.75.

List the parts needed so links to partitioning can be made, e.g. 3.75 = 3 + 0.7 + 0.05.

In pairs, give children a number strip and paper clips.

Given that the number strip represents 3 to 4 kg, ask about the positions 3.5 kg, 3.25 kg and 3.75 kg using the clips.

Confirm positions by looking at the value of each digit in the number and linking to the fractions $\frac{1}{2}$, $\frac{1}{4}$ and $\frac{3}{4}$.

Pose the problem that the number strip now represents 4 to 5 kg.

*What does each paper clip represent now?*

*What can we use to help us?*

*How much more is 3.75 kg than 3.25 kg?*

Discuss how much more we need to add to each mass to equal 4 kg. Link to complements to 100 using number bonds. Look at rounding to the nearest whole kg.

Ask children to find other masses that would go between paper clips. Try to find the positions of, say, 3.2 kg, 3.4 kg, 3.6 kg and 3.8 kg, linking this to fifths.

**ANSWERS**

**Task A: 1)** E.g. the paper clip is less than $\frac{1}{4}$ of the way along the scale **2)** 1.2 kg **3)** Children's recording to show 1.4 kg on the fourth mark and 1.6 kg on the sixth mark **4)** 0.15 kg **5)** 1.8 kg = 1 kg + 0.8 kg **6)** 0.2 kg

**Task B: 1)** 2.25 kg **2)** 3.65 kg **3)** 0.75 kg **4)** 0.35 kg **5)** 2.25 kg, 2.3 kg, 3.65 kg **6)** 1.35 kg

**Task C: 1)** 2.7 kg **2)** 2.45 kg **3)** 0.3 kg **4)** 0.55 kg **5)** 2.45 kg, 2.55 kg, 2.7 kg **6)** In order: 2 kg, 3 kg, 3 kg

# Task A (Independent task or guided learning with an adult)

**1)** Tim says that the paper clip shows 1.25 kg. How can you explain to Tim that he has made a mistake?

**2)** What does the paper clip show?

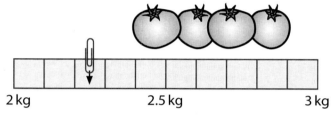

1 kg          2 kg

**3)** Show where 1.4 kg and 1.6 kg will be on this scale.

**4)** How many more kilograms (kg) is 1.75 kg than 1.6 kg?

**5)** Tim weighs 1.8 kg of bananas. He records this as 1.8 kg = 1 kg + 8 kg. Correct his mistake.

**6)** Use the scale to work out how many more kilograms of bananas he will need to reach 2 kg.

# Task B (Independent task)

Pete is weighing tomatoes and carrots.

He uses his number strip and paper clip to show what happened.

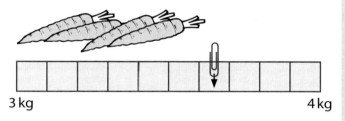

2 kg          2.5 kg          3 kg

**1)** How many kilograms (kg) of tomatoes does he have?

**2)** How many kilograms (kg) of carrots does he have?

**3)** How many more kilograms of tomatoes does he need to reach 3 kg?

**4)** How many more kilograms of carrots does he need to reach 4 kg?

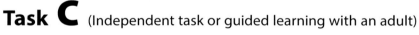

**5)** Pete also weighs 2.3 kg of potatoes. Put all the amounts in order from lightest to heaviest.

3 kg          4 kg

**6)** How much heavier are the carrots than the potatoes?

# Task C (Independent task or guided learning with an adult)

Izzy is weighing potatoes and carrots.

She uses her number strip and paper clip to show what happened.

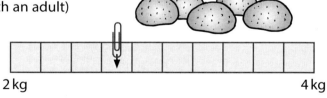

2 kg          4 kg

**1)** How many kilograms (kg) of potatoes does she have?

**2)** How many kilograms (kg) of carrots does she have?

**3)** How many more kilograms of potatoes does she need to reach 3 kg?

**4)** How many more kilograms of carrots does she need to reach 3 kg?

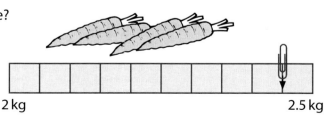

2 kg          2.5 kg

**5)** Izzy also weighs 2.55 kg of cabbages. Order all the vegetables from lightest to heaviest.

**HINT:** Check the scale each time.

**6)** Now round the mass of each vegetable to the nearest kilogram.

# UNIT 14  Solving problems about fractions and decimals

## National Curriculum link:
**Solve simple measure and money problems involving fractions and decimals to two decimal places.**

## Year 4 pupils should already know that:
- Decimals and fractions are different ways of expressing numbers and proportions
- There is a clear link between division and fractional representations
- The positions of the digits in a decimal number show the value of each digit

## Supporting understanding
Measurement provides a useful context for exploring decimals. In this unit, children will work with length and consider fractions or decimal fractions of a metre.

Each 10 cm is $\frac{1}{10}$ of a metre or 0.1 m and every 1 cm is $\frac{1}{100}$ of a metre (or $\frac{1}{10}$ of 10 cm) and is shown as 0.01 cm.

Measurements can be recorded by partitioning to show place value.

E.g. $3.25 \text{ m} = 3 \text{ m} + \frac{2}{10} \text{ m} + \frac{5}{100} \text{ m} = 3 \text{ m} + \frac{25}{100} \text{ m}$

and $3.25 \text{ m} = 3 \text{ m} + 0.2 \text{ m} + 0.05 \text{ m} = 3 \text{ m} + 0.25 \text{ m}$.

## Contextualising mathematics
For children to understand why they are learning the mathematics in the curriculum, it is important that they see how concepts are connected and their purpose in real-life contexts.

Raising the profile of mathematics across the curriculum helps to develop these contexts for children. They can also see how the mathematics they learn in the mathematics classroom can be applied in other subjects.

Measurement and statistics are particularly useful to explore.

### ANSWERS
**Task A: 1)** E.g. concrete 1.5 m = $1 + \frac{5}{10}$ m (test 1) and 1.9 m = 1 m $+ \frac{9}{10}$ m (test 2) so 1.5 m < 1.9 m **2)** $\frac{2}{10}$ **3)** 1.4 m **Challenge:** Concrete
**Task B: 1)** E.g. soil 0.37 m = $\frac{3}{10} + \frac{7}{100}$ or $\frac{37}{100}$ m (test 1) and 0.42 = $\frac{4}{10}$ $+ \frac{2}{100}$ or $\frac{42}{100}$ m (test 2) so 0.37 m < 0.42 m **2)** 1.69 m **3)** Carpet 0.9 m or 1.5 m and grass 0.6 m or 1.2 m
**Task C:** In order: 0.46 m, 0.64 m, 1.45 m, 1.5 m, 1.75 m, 1.85 m

|   | Carpet | Plastic | Wood | Grass | Concrete | Soil |
|---|--------|---------|------|-------|----------|------|
| 2 | **1.5 m** | 1.69 m | 1.6 m | **0.64 m** | 1.9 m | 0.42 m |
| 3 | 1.8 m | **1.75 m** | **1.85 m** | 0.75 m | **1.45 m** | **0.46 m** |

## In the classroom

Introduce the problem that will be developed throughout the lesson:

*Children are investigating the distance a toy car rolls on different surfaces.*

*Here are the results after the first test:*

|        | Carpet | Concrete | Wood | Grass | Plastic |
|--------|--------|----------|------|-------|---------|
| Test 1 | 1.2 m  | 1.5 m    | 1.8 m | 0.9 m |         |

*Use the information to make up some statements about the first test. The words 'further', 'less than' and 'more than' will help you.*

Ask children to prepare to prove their statements.

Take feedback and make some comparisons.

*We do not yet know the result for plastic.*

Pose these, or similar, questions for different groups to consider and prove in their own way:

- *Do you think that the car went further than 1.2 m on plastic? Why? What would be a good estimate?*

- *What if the result for plastic is $\frac{2}{10}$ m more than for wood? What measurement would it be?*

- *What if the result for plastic is the midway measurement between the results for concrete and wood?*

Explore possibilities and proofs that children have used.

Reveal that the result for plastic is 1.65 m. Show this as:

$1.65 \text{ m} = 1 \text{ m} + \frac{6}{10} \text{ m} + \frac{5}{100} \text{ m}$ or $1 \text{ m} + \frac{65}{100} \text{ m}$ and

$1.65 \text{ m} = 1 \text{ m} + 0.6 \text{ m} + 0.05 \text{ m}$ or $1 \text{ m} + 0.65 \text{ m}$

*On which surface did the car go furthest in test 1?*

Children will explore tests 2 and 3 in their independent tasks.

## Task A (Guided learning with an adult)

1) Compare the results for test 1 and test 2 for each of these surfaces:

   **a)** concrete **b)** grass **c)** plastic

   Record the value of each digit by partitioning and then use the < symbol.

|        | Carpet | Concrete | Wood  | Grass | Plastic |
|--------|--------|----------|-------|-------|---------|
| Test 1 | 1.2 m  | 1.5 m    | 1.8 m | 0.9 m | 1.65 m  |
| Test 2 |        | 1.9 m    | 1.6 m | 0.6 m | 1.69 m  |

2) The result for test 1 on the wood surface was more than test 2. How many tenths more?

3) The car on the carpet went $\frac{2}{10}$ m further in test 2. How far did it go?

**Challenge:**

On which surface did the car go furthest in test 2?

## Task B (Independent task)

1) Compare the results in each test for the wood, concrete and then the soil surface.

|        | Carpet | Plastic | Wood  | Grass | Concrete | Soil   |
|--------|--------|---------|-------|-------|----------|--------|
| Test 1 | 1.2 m  | 1.65 m  | 1.8 m | 0.9 m | 1.5 m    | 0.37 m |
| Test 2 |        |         | 1.6 m |       | 1.9 m    | 0.42 m |

   Record the value of each digit by partitioning and then use the < symbol.

2) The car on the plastic surface in test 2 went 4 cm further than in test 1. How far did it go in test 2?

3) The difference between tests 1 and 2 for both the grass and carpet was $\frac{3}{10}$ m. What are the possible results for test 2? There is more than one solution.

## Task C (Independent task)

Use the clues to help fill in the missing results.

|        | Carpet | Plastic | Wood  | Grass  | Concrete | Soil   |
|--------|--------|---------|-------|--------|----------|--------|
| Test 1 | 1.2 m  | 1.65 m  | 1.8 m | 0.9 m  | 1.5 m    | 0.37 m |
| Test 2 |        | 1.69 m  | 1.6 m |        | 1.9 m    | 0.42 m |
| Test 3 | 1.8 m  |         |       | 0.75 m |          |        |

- The missing result for the carpet is the midway point between the results for test 1 and 3.

- The missing result for plastic is less than 10 cm more than 1.69 m but has an odd number of hundredths.

- The missing result for wood is 25 cm more than in test 2.

- The missing result for concrete is the sum of $1\frac{1}{4}$ m and $\frac{1}{5}$ m.

- The missing result for plastic is 30 cm more than the missing result for concrete.

- The missing result for soil can be shown as $\frac{46}{100}$ m and the missing result for grass as $\frac{64}{100}$ m.

- Now write all the missing results in order from smallest to largest.

# Finding unit fractions of quantities

## National Curriculum link:

**Solve problems involving increasingly harder fractions to calculate quantities, and fractions to divide quantities,** including non-unit fractions where the answer is a whole number.

## Year 4 pupils should already know that:

- Unit fractions all have numerators with the value of 1
- The denominator determines the number of equal parts there are in the whole
- We use division to help us work with fractions
- Calculations such as $40 \div 4 = 10$ can be written as $\frac{1}{4}$ of $40 = 10$ and vice versa

## Supporting understanding

Children will grasp this concept more easily if they have previously experienced the 'whole' as not necessarily being 'one'.

To find the fraction of an amount or a set of objects, we must view the set as the 'whole', i.e. the whole amount or whole set.

Fraction bars and other images can be used to show how the 'whole' can be split into fractions.

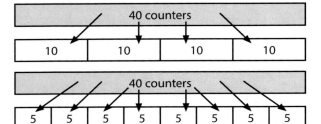

## Resources to help to find fractions of a quantity

Cuisenaire rods or integer bars are useful for children to explore fractional parts of quantities.

For example, to find $\frac{1}{5}$ of 20 we can take two '10' rods to represent 20. Remembering that fifths arise from dividing the whole into five equal parts, we must look for five identical smaller rods that have the same value as the whole, i.e. 20.

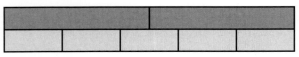

20 divided by 5 is 4 so $\frac{1}{5}$ of 20 is 4.

**ANSWERS**

**Task A: 1)** $\frac{1}{4}$ of 16 = 4 and $\frac{1}{4}$ of 32 = 8 and then 16 ÷ 4 = 4 and 32 ÷ 4 = 8 **2)** $\frac{1}{4}$ of 32 is double $\frac{1}{4}$ of 16, as 32 is double 16 **3)** $\frac{1}{8}$ of 16 = 2 and $\frac{1}{8}$ of 32 = 4 and then 16 ÷ 8 = 2 and 32 ÷ 8 = 4; the answers for $\frac{1}{8}$ are half those for $\frac{1}{4}$ **Challenge:** 24, because it is in the multiplication table of 4

**Tasks B and C:** E.g. $\frac{1}{5}$ of 35 = 7 and 35 ÷ 5 = 7

## In the classroom

Revisit the key point that the denominator shows the number of equal parts there are in the whole.

Check that children are secure with this by asking about the number of parts the whole has been divided into for thirds, fifths, tenths, hundredths, etc.

Explain that knowledge of division can also help us when we are trying to find a fraction of a set of objects.

*The set of objects can be described as the whole.*

*Consider a set of 40 objects, such as counters. This is the whole. I want to find a quarter of the whole set.*

*What should I do?*

Ask children to discuss the problem and make suggestions.

Establish that we can find a quarter by dividing by 4.

Use the visual representation of the whole (as shown on the left) and / or Cuisenaire rods or integer bars to model dividing into four equal parts, e.g. sharing 40 between 4.

Using a language structure, establish that:
*'One quarter of 40 is 10, as 40 divided by 4 is 10.'*

Revisit the key point that this calculation can be written as $\frac{1}{4}$ of 40 = 10 or 40 ÷ 4 = 10.

*We can also find a quarter by halving a half.*

Focus on the use of multiplication and division facts to help identify fractions of a whole set.

Pose these, or similar, questions for different groups to consider:

- *I know the 8 times table. What fractions will this help me with?*

- *What multiplication fact should I use to find $\frac{1}{8}$ of 40?*

- *I used the division fact 32 ÷ 8 = 4 to help me find a fraction of a whole set. What was I trying to find out?*

- *How can we use what we know about quarters and halves to help us find eighths?*

# Task A (Independent task)

Use Cuisenaire rods, integer bars or similar to explore these quantities:

**1)** Find a quarter $\left(\frac{1}{4}\right)$ of 16 and then a quarter of 32.

Record your work as a number sentence using the division sign.

**2)** What patterns do you notice?

**3)** Now find an eighth $\left(\frac{1}{8}\right)$ of 16 and then an eighth of 32.

Record your work in the same way. Do you notice any other patterns?

**Challenge:**

Would it be easier to find a quarter $\left(\frac{1}{4}\right)$ of 24 or of 25? Why?

Have a go and record what you find out.

| **16** |
| --- |

| **32** |
| --- |

# Task B (Independent task)

Use Cuisenaire rods, integer bars or the image used in the lesson to help you.

- Roll the dice to make fractions, e.g. a  makes a fifth.
  Make a tenth if you roll a one.
- Think about the multiplication table that will help you with your fraction.
- Choose a number from the grid for your whole.
- Now find your fraction of this whole.
- Record your calculation,
  e.g. $\frac{1}{4}$ of 40 = 10 and 40 ÷ 4 = 10.

**HINT:** You may find this language useful: One quarter of 40 is 10 as 40 divided by 4 is 10.

| 18 | 35 | 16 |
| --- | --- | --- |
| 32 | 24 | 30 |
| 40 | 36 | ? |

You choose!

# Task C (Independent task)

Use the image used in the lesson and your division facts to help you.

- Spin a paperclip round a pencil on the octagon spinner to give you a fraction.
- Think about the multiplication table that will help you with your fraction.
- Choose a number from the grid for your whole.
- Now find your fraction of this whole.
- Record your calculation, e.g. $\frac{1}{4}$ of 48 = ___ and 48 ÷ 4 = ___ .

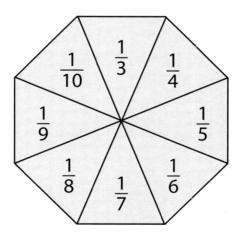

| 48 | 35 | 56 |
| --- | --- | --- |
| 36 | 100 | 60 |
| 27 | 64 | ? |

You choose!

# UNIT 16  Solving problems about unit fractions of quantities

## National Curriculum link:

**Solve problems involving increasingly harder fractions to calculate quantities, and fractions to divide quantities**, including non-unit fractions where the answer is a whole number.

## Year 4 pupils should already know that:

- The denominator determines the number of equal parts there are in the whole
- We use division to help us work with fractions
- Calculations such as 40 ÷ 4 = 10 can be written as $\frac{1}{4}$ of 40 = 10 and vice versa

## Supporting understanding

In Unit 15, children began to explore unit fractions of a set. They made links to multiplication and division facts to help make decisions.

Making links using language structures helps to reinforce this relationship.

> One sixth of **18** is **3** as
> **18** divided by **6** is **3**.

The language structure will continue to support understanding in this unit. This builds on a Year 3 objective.

## Recognising fractions of a set

Resources such as Cuisenaire rods or integer bars are useful as a starting point here.

Imagine that we want to identify what fraction 6 is of 30. By representing the whole and the six, children can explore how many of the six rods equal the whole.

| 30 |
|---|

| 6 |
|---|

| 6 | 6 | 6 | 6 | 6 |
|---|---|---|---|---|

In doing so, we find that 6 represents $\frac{1}{5}$ of 30. We can also use the grouping model of division to confirm that 30 ÷ 5 = 6 or there are five groups of 6 in 30.

### ANSWERS
**Task A:** $\frac{1}{2}$ of 30 = 15, $\frac{1}{3}$ of 30 = 10 and $\frac{1}{6}$ of 30 = 5 **Challenge:** $\frac{1}{10}$
**Task B: 1)** $\frac{1}{4}$ of 48 = 12, $\frac{1}{6}$ of 48 = 8, $\frac{1}{8}$ of 48 = 6, $\frac{1}{12}$ of 48 = 4, with related division facts, e.g. 48 ÷ 4 = 12 **2)** $\frac{1}{4}$; 60 ÷ 4 = 15
**Task C: 1)** $\frac{1}{9}$ of 9 = 1, $\frac{1}{9}$ of 18 = 2, $\frac{1}{9}$ of 27 = 3, etc. **2)** 36 = $\frac{1}{2}$ of 72, 24 = $\frac{1}{3}$ of 72, 18 = $\frac{1}{4}$ of 72, 12 = $\frac{1}{6}$ of 72, 8 = $\frac{1}{9}$ of 72, etc.

## In the classroom

> Revisit the language: '*One sixth of **18** is **3** as **18** divided by **6** is **3**.*'
> *How can we prove this is correct?*
> *What can we visualise or draw?*

> Introduce the problem that will be developed during the lesson:
> - *Children in Class 4 are decorating their model rockets.*
> - *There are different boxes of stickers in the art cupboard.*
>
>
>
> - *Beth decides to use $\frac{1}{3}$ of a box.*

> Pose these, or similar, questions for different groups to consider:
> - *How many moon stickers is this?*
> - *If she chooses stars, how many more stickers will she have than if she chooses moons?*
> - *How many sun stickers is this?*

> Return to the language structure and the fraction bar images used in Unit 15 to confirm answers to the previous questions, e.g. '*One third of 30 is 10 as 30 divided by 3 is 10.*'

> Ashton only uses six stickers.
> - *We know that Beth uses $\frac{1}{3}$ of a box. What do we need to find out about Ashton's stickers?*
> - *What different fractions of each box could this be?*

> Use a visual such as a Cuisenaire rod or integer bar to represent 30 as the whole. What fraction of 30 is 6?
> Ask children to discuss what we can do to help us.
> Model finding how many sixes there are in 30.
> *We now have five equal parts and we know that a whole divided into five equal parts shows fifths.*
> *So 6 is $\frac{1}{5}$ of 30.*

# Task A (Independent task)

Jade wants to use some moon stickers, but she cannot decide what fraction to use.
Use what you know about sharing to find out how many stickers she could use.
Write the fraction each time.

| 30 stickers ☾ |

**Challenge:**
What fraction of 30 is 3?

**HINT:** You can use cubes, Cuisenaire rods or integer bars to help you.

# Task B (Independent task)

**1)** Help Pete to find out how many sun stickers he can put on his rocket if he uses the following fractions:
$\frac{1}{4}$  $\frac{1}{6}$  $\frac{1}{8}$  $\frac{1}{12}$
Write the division facts that helped you.

**2)** Pete also decides to use 15 star stickers.
What fraction of the whole box is this?
Show how you worked this out.

# Task C (Independent task)

Sami and Izzy are also decorating their rockets.

**1)** Sami uses $\frac{1}{9}$ of the lightning bolt stickers.
Investigate to find out how many stickers Sami uses and how many stickers were in the full box.
How many different answers can you find?
Write your answers as $\frac{1}{9}$ of ___ = ___ .

**2)** Izzy uses a fraction of the planet stickers. She uses an even number of these stickers.
How many stickers could she use? Is there more than one solution?
What fraction of 72 is this?

# UNIT 17 Non-unit fractions of quantities

## National Curriculum link:

**Solve problems involving increasingly harder fractions to calculate quantities, and fractions to divide quantities, including non-unit fractions where the answer is a whole number.**

## Year 4 pupils should already know that:

- Non-unit fractions do not have a numerator of 1
- We use division and multiplication to find a non-unit fraction of an amount or set of objects
- The denominator determines the number of equal parts the whole is divided into and the numerator shows how many of these equal parts are represented by the fraction

## Supporting understanding

Language structures, such as the example shown here, can support children to make sense of the fractions they are working with.

> It is a fraction with **8** equal parts. I have **5** of the parts. I have $\frac{5}{8}$.

The language can be developed for mixed numbers as: *There are 2 wholes and a fraction with 8 equal parts. I have 5 of the parts. I have 2 and $\frac{5}{8}$.*

## Non-unit fractions of a set or quantity

Children will need to 'understand the relation between non-unit fractions and multiplication and division of quantities, with particular emphasis on tenths and hundredths'.

Images used previously that support children to find a unit fraction of an amount provide the platform for recognising and working with non-unit fractions.

$\frac{1}{4}$ of 40 or 40 ÷ 4 = 10

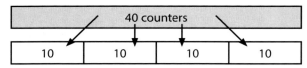

Now we can count in quarters along the bar to establish that $\frac{1}{4}$ of 40 is 10, $\frac{2}{4}$ of 40 is 20 and $\frac{3}{4}$ of 40 is 30.

**ANSWERS**
**Task A: 1)** 6 litres **2)** 12 litres **3)** 15 litres **4)** 18 litres **5)** $\frac{1}{2}$; $\frac{2}{4}$ is the same as $\frac{1}{2}$
**Task B: 1)** 6 litres $\left(\frac{3}{10}\right)$ and 14 litres $\left(\frac{7}{10}\right)$ **2)** 12 litres $\left(\frac{3}{10}\right)$ and 28 litres $\left(\frac{7}{10}\right)$ **3)** 30 litres $\left(\frac{3}{10}\right)$ and 70 litres $\left(\frac{7}{10}\right)$ **4)** 15 litres $\left(\frac{3}{10}\right)$ and 35 litres $\frac{7}{10}$ **5)** 6 litres $\left(\frac{3}{10}$ of 20$\right)$ and 14 litres $\left(\frac{7}{10}$ of 20$\right)$ sum to 20 litres, which is $\frac{10}{10}$ or the whole; it is also true for 40 litres as 12 litres and 28 litres sum to 40 litres, which is the whole $\left(\frac{10}{10}\right)$
**Task C:** E.g. $\frac{7}{100}$ of 400 litres = 28 litres, $\frac{7}{8}$ of 400 litres = 350 litres, $\frac{7}{10}$ of 400 litres = 280 litres; $\frac{7}{8}$ of 64 litres = 56 litres **Challenge:** E.g. 160 litres $\left(\frac{7}{8}$ and $\frac{7}{10}\right)$, 1200 litres (all three fractions, since 1200 is a multiple of 400); some children may go further and suggest answers that are not whole, e.g. $\frac{7}{100}$ of 160 litres = 11$\frac{2}{10}$ or 11.2 litres

## In the classroom

> Revisit the key point that non-unit fractions do not have a numerator of 1.

> Ask children to quickly write down a non-unit fraction that they know and sketch an image to represent it.

> They should practise the language: *It is a fraction with **5** equal parts. I have **3** of the parts.* to describe their fraction for their partner to identify ($\frac{3}{5}$).

> Use the fraction $\frac{3}{4}$ to pose this problem:
> *Zack needs to find $\frac{3}{4}$ of 40 litres. He knows how to find $\frac{1}{4}$ but is not sure how to find $\frac{3}{4}$.*
> *What do you think he should do? Why?*

> Use the image (left) or similar to establish that to find $\frac{3}{4}$ we must use division to help find $\frac{1}{4}$ first.
> *Now we know the value of $\frac{1}{4}$ we can count along to find the value of $\frac{3}{4}$.*
> Agree that we have used division to find $\frac{1}{4}$ and then multiplication to find $\frac{3}{4}$.
> The language structure can be adapted to help children make sense of this: *'There are **4** equal parts of **10** litres and I have **3** of the parts. I have $\frac{3}{4}$ of **40** litres, which is **30** litres.'*

> Choose two other fractions from the examples children made earlier, or use $\frac{2}{5}$ and $\frac{5}{8}$:
> $\frac{3}{4}$ of 12 litres $\quad$ $\frac{2}{5}$ of 15 litres $\quad$ $\frac{5}{8}$ of 24 litres
> Ask different groups to find these fractions of amounts ($\frac{5}{8}$ being the most challenging and $\frac{3}{4}$ the least).
> Ask children to use images and language structures to prove their solutions. Discuss that it is easier to find fractions of an amount when the amount is a multiple of the denominator.

# Task **A** (Independent task)

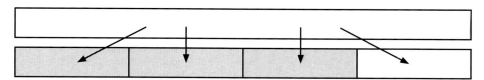

Find $\frac{3}{4}$ of these amounts.

**1)** 8 litres

**2)** 16 litres

**3)** 20 litres

**4)** 24 litres

**5)** Zack also found $\frac{2}{4}$ of these amounts. His friend got exactly the same answers as Zack, but he did not use $\frac{2}{4}$. What fraction did he use? How do you know?

# Task **B** (Independent task)

There are **10** equal parts of ____ litres and I have **3** of the parts.

Find $\frac{3}{10}$ and $\frac{7}{10}$ of these amounts.

**1)** 20 litres

**2)** 40 litres

**3)** 100 litres

**4)** 50 litres

**5)** What happens when you add together $\frac{3}{10}$ of 20 litres and $\frac{7}{10}$ of 20 litres? Why is this? Is it also true for $\frac{3}{10}$ of 40 litres and $\frac{7}{10}$ of 40 litres?

# Task **C** (Independent task)

Find $\frac{7}{8}$, $\frac{7}{10}$ or $\frac{7}{100}$ of these amounts.

- Choose a capacity from the grid.
- Think about your division facts to help you decide what fraction to choose.
- Find this fraction of the amount.
- Is it possible to use each capacity more than once with a different fraction?

| | | |
|---|---|---|
| 400 litres | 64 litres | 300 litres |
| 800 litres | 120 litres | 80 litres |
| 90 litres | 40 litres | ? |

**Challenge:**

Find other capacities for **?** where two or all three fractions can be used easily.

# UNIT 18  Adding fractions with the same denominator

## National Curriculum link:

**Add** and subtract **fractions with the same denominator.**

## Year 4 pupils should already know that:

- A whole can also be described as a fraction, e.g. fifths means there are five equal parts so the whole can be described as $\frac{5}{5}$
- It is much easier to add fractions when the denominators are the same

## Supporting understanding

In previous units, children have counted in different fraction steps, including hundredths. Images have been used to support this understanding.

Fraction bars can be used to support counting on. They also support the transition to number lines, e.g. $\frac{3}{7} + \frac{2}{7}$:

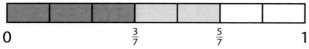

It is also vital that children have a secure understanding that a 'whole' can be represented as a fraction, e.g. $\frac{70}{100} + \frac{30}{100}$ is $\frac{100}{100}$, which is equal to 1.

## Recording addition calculations on the number line

We can show calculations with fractions on a number line in the same way that we do with whole numbers.

Consider the addition $\frac{5}{8} + \frac{2}{8}$.

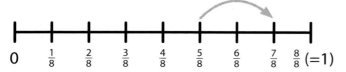

The number line will also support calculations that bridge the whole, e.g. $\frac{5}{8} + \frac{4}{8}$, by partitioning $\frac{4}{8}$ into $\frac{3}{8}$ (to complete the whole) and $\frac{1}{8}$.

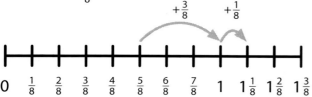

## In the classroom

Show several different fraction bars; fifths, sixths, eighths, tenths and twelfths would be useful here.

Invite children to choose one of the bars (or visualise one of their own) and practise counting in these fraction steps up to and beyond one.

Pose these, or similar, questions for different groups to consider:

- *After you have counted your third fraction step, how many more steps must you take to complete the whole (or the next whole)?*
  *What addition sentence can you write?*

- *I only need to count on five steps to complete my whole. What fraction did I start on? What did I count on? Find some different possibilities and write addition sentences.*

Also consider examples beyond 1, e.g. from $1\frac{1}{6}$, count on $\frac{5}{6}$ to complete the second whole.

Revisit the key point that it is much easier to count in or add fractions when the denominators are the same.

*Which is easier: $\frac{5}{8} + \frac{2}{8}$ or $\frac{3}{8} + \frac{1}{5}$?*

Model $\frac{5}{8} + \frac{2}{8}$ on a fraction bar and then as jumps on the number line.

Reinforce this by asking children to show one of their own fraction additions on a number line.

Ask children to consider the addition calculation $\frac{5}{8} + \frac{4}{8}$ and count in fraction steps from $\frac{5}{8}$ along a fraction bar.

*What is different this time? What can we use to help us?*

Add another fraction bar so that the count can be continued beyond 1; cover the completed whole with a 'whole' to help make sense of the mixed number. Model this on the number line, showing how the whole is bridged using partitioning and knowledge of bonds to the whole (as shown on the left).

### ANSWERS

**Task A:** 1) $\frac{7}{8}$ 2) $\frac{8}{8}$ or 1 3) $1\frac{1}{8}$ 4) $1\frac{1}{8}$ 5) $1\frac{2}{8}$ 6) $1\frac{2}{8}$ 7) E.g. $\frac{7}{8} + \frac{4}{8} = 1\frac{3}{8}$

**Task B:** Number lines for answers: 1) $\frac{9}{10}$ 2) $\frac{5}{8}$ 3) $1\frac{1}{7}$ 4) $\frac{4}{6}$ 5) $\frac{80}{100}$ 6) $\frac{7}{8}$
7) $\frac{3}{5} + \frac{4}{5}$ (or $\frac{2}{5} + \frac{2}{5}$) 8) $\frac{3}{7} + \frac{6}{7}$ (or $\frac{4}{7} + \frac{2}{7}$)

**Task C:** Number lines for answers: 1) $1\frac{2}{9}$ 2) $\frac{3}{9}$ 3) $\frac{7}{8}$ 4) $1\frac{2}{7}$ 5) $1\frac{2}{6}$
6) $\frac{95}{100}$ 7) $1\frac{2}{6}$
$+ \frac{5}{6}$ (or $\frac{4}{6} + \frac{1}{6}$) 8) E.g. $\frac{5}{7} + \frac{3}{7} + \frac{4}{7} = 1\frac{5}{7}$; it could not be $\frac{5}{6} + \frac{3}{6} + \frac{4}{6}$ as this is equal to 2; it cannot have any denominator less than 7

## Task **A** (Independent task or guided learning with an adult)

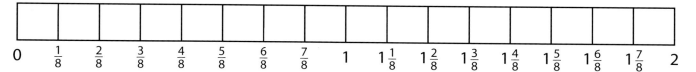

| | | | | | | | | | | | | | | | |

0   $\frac{1}{8}$   $\frac{2}{8}$   $\frac{3}{8}$   $\frac{4}{8}$   $\frac{5}{8}$   $\frac{6}{8}$   $\frac{7}{8}$   1   $1\frac{1}{8}$   $1\frac{2}{8}$   $1\frac{3}{8}$   $1\frac{4}{8}$   $1\frac{5}{8}$   $1\frac{6}{8}$   $1\frac{7}{8}$   2

Copy and complete the calculations:

**1)** $\frac{4}{8} + \frac{3}{8} = $ ____

**2)** $\frac{5}{8} + \frac{3}{8} = $ ____

**3)** $\frac{6}{8} + \frac{3}{8} = $ ____

**4)** $\frac{7}{8} + \frac{2}{8} = $ ____

**5)** $\frac{7}{8} + \frac{3}{8} = $ ____

**6)** $\frac{6}{8} + \frac{4}{8} = $ ____

**7)** Now make up some more addition calculations of your own.

## Task **B** (Independent task or guided learning with an adult)

Show the following calculations on a number line:

**1)** $\frac{7}{10} + \frac{2}{10} = $ ____

**2)** $\frac{3}{8} + $ ____ $= 1$

**3)** $\frac{4}{7} + \frac{4}{7} = $ ____

**4)** ____ $+ \frac{3}{6} = 1\frac{1}{6}$

**5)** $\frac{50}{100} + \frac{30}{100} = $ ____

**6)** $\frac{3}{8} + $ ____ $= 1\frac{2}{8}$

What calculations do these number lines show?

**7)**

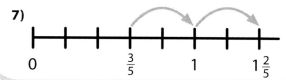

0          $\frac{3}{5}$          1          $1\frac{2}{5}$

**8)**

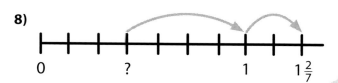

0          ?          1          $1\frac{2}{7}$

## Task **C** (Independent task)

Show the following calculations on a number line:

**1)** $\frac{5}{9} + \frac{6}{9} = $ ____

**2)** $\frac{8}{9} + $ ____ $= 1\frac{2}{9}$

**3)** $\frac{5}{8} + \frac{4}{8} + $ ____ $= 2$

**4)** ____ $+ \frac{2}{7} = 1\frac{4}{7}$

**5)** $\frac{5}{6} + \frac{1}{2} = $ ____

**6)** ____ $+ \frac{7}{100} = 1\frac{2}{100}$

**7)** What calculation does this number line show?

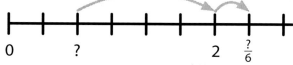

0          ?                    2     $\frac{?}{6}$

**8)** Tom drew a number line for this calculation: $\frac{5}{?} + \frac{3}{?} + \frac{4}{?}$.
His answer is less than 2.
What could his calculation be? What could it not be? Why?

# UNIT 19  Subtracting fractions with the same denominator

## National Curriculum link:

Add and **subtract fractions with the same denominator.**

## Year 4 pupils should already know that:

- A whole can also be described as a fraction, e.g. fifths means there are five equal parts so the whole can be described as $\frac{5}{5}$
- It is much easier to subtract fractions when the denominators are the same

## Supporting understanding

In previous units, children have been counting on and back in fraction steps. They have been using fraction bars and number lines for addition.

We can use similar images for subtraction, using the fraction bar as a transitional image, e.g. $\frac{9}{10} - \frac{4}{10} = \frac{5}{10}$:

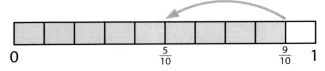

## Recording subtraction calculations on the number line

We can show subtraction calculations with fractions on a number line in the same way that we do with whole numbers.

Consider the subtraction $\frac{7}{8} - \frac{3}{8}$:

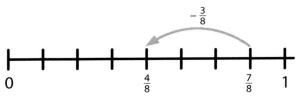

The number line will also support calculations that bridge the whole, e.g. $1\frac{2}{8} - \frac{3}{8}$, by partitioning $\frac{3}{8}$ into $\frac{2}{8}$ (to reach the whole) and $\frac{1}{8}$:

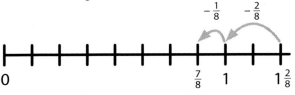

**ANSWERS**

**Task A: 1)** $\frac{7}{8}$ **2)** $\frac{3}{8}$ **3)** $\frac{2}{8}$ **4)** $\frac{7}{8}$ **5)** $\frac{6}{8}$ **6)** $\frac{7}{8}$ **7)** E.g. $1\frac{3}{8} - \frac{4}{8} = \frac{7}{8}$

**Task B: Number lines for answers: 1)** $\frac{1}{10}$ **2)** $\frac{5}{6}$ **3)** $\frac{6}{7}$ **4)** $\frac{4}{5}$ (this is a simple calculation as $\frac{5}{5}$ is 1) **5)** $\frac{4}{6}$ **6)** $1\frac{2}{10}$ **7)** $1\frac{2}{5} - \frac{4}{5} = \frac{3}{5}$ **8)** $1\frac{2}{6} - \frac{5}{6} = \frac{3}{6}$

**Task C: Number lines for answers: 1)** $\frac{2}{8}$ **2)** $\frac{6}{9}$ **3)** $1\frac{7}{10}$ **4)** $\frac{8}{10}$ **5)** $\frac{3}{6}$ **6)** $2\frac{1}{8}$ **7)** $2\frac{2}{7} - \frac{7}{7}$ (1) = $1\frac{2}{8}$ **8)** E.g. $2 - \frac{6}{10} = 1\frac{4}{10}$, $2\frac{1}{9} - \frac{6}{9} = 1\frac{4}{9}$, $2\frac{2}{8} - \frac{6}{8} = 1\frac{4}{8}$, $2\frac{3}{7} - \frac{6}{7} = 1\frac{4}{7}$

## In the classroom

Using a visual, practise counting on and back in fraction steps beyond 1.

Stop at different points and ask questions such as: *How many more eighths must we count back to return to two?*

Link this to whole numbers.

---

Continue by asking questions that require counting in tenths, e.g:

- *I start on $\frac{7}{10}$ and count back $\frac{3}{10}$. Where do I land? What subtraction sentence can you write?*

- *I counted back $\frac{4}{10}$ and landed on $\frac{2}{10}$. Where did I start? What subtraction sentence can you write?*

- *I started on $\frac{9}{10}$ and landed on an odd number of tenths. What fraction did I subtract and what fraction did I land on? Find some different possibilities and write subtraction sentences.*

---

Revisit the key point that it is much easier to count back or subtract fractions when the denominators are the same.

*Which is easier: $\frac{7}{8} - \frac{3}{8}$ or $\frac{7}{8} - \frac{1}{3}$?*

Model $\frac{7}{8} - \frac{3}{8}$ on a fraction bar and then as jumps on the number line.

Reinforce this by asking children to show their subtraction sentence, e.g. $\frac{7}{10} - \frac{3}{10}$, on a number line.

---

Ask children to consider the following subtraction calculation: $1\frac{2}{8} - \frac{3}{8}$:

*How can we use the fraction bars this time? Where do we need to start? (We need two bars.)*

Count back $\frac{3}{8}$, but emphasise that we count back $\frac{2}{8}$ to reach 1 and then a further $\frac{1}{8}$. It is useful to exchange the whole bar for an eighths bar to continue the count.

Model this on the number line, showing how the whole is bridged using partitioning (as shown on the left).

## Task **A** (Independent task)

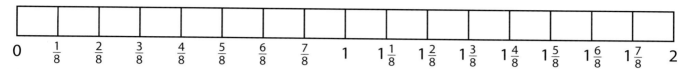

| 0 | $\frac{1}{8}$ | $\frac{2}{8}$ | $\frac{3}{8}$ | $\frac{4}{8}$ | $\frac{5}{8}$ | $\frac{6}{8}$ | $\frac{7}{8}$ | 1 | $1\frac{1}{8}$ | $1\frac{2}{8}$ | $1\frac{3}{8}$ | $1\frac{4}{8}$ | $1\frac{5}{8}$ | $1\frac{6}{8}$ | $1\frac{7}{8}$ | 2 |

Copy and complete the calculations:

**1)** $\frac{8}{8} - \frac{1}{8} = $ ____

**2)** $\frac{7}{8} - \frac{4}{8} = $ ____

**3)** $\frac{7}{8} - \frac{5}{8} = $ ____

**4)** $1\frac{1}{8} - \frac{2}{8} = $ ____

**5)** $1\frac{1}{8} - \frac{3}{8} = $ ____

**6)** $1\frac{2}{8} - \frac{3}{8} = $ ____

**7)** Now make up some more subtraction calculations of your own.

## Task **B** (Guided learning with an adult)

Show the following calculations on a number line:

**1)** $\frac{7}{10} - \frac{6}{10} = $ ____

**2)** $\frac{5}{6} - $ ____ $ = 0$

**3)** $1\frac{1}{7} - \frac{2}{7} = $ ____

**4)** $1\frac{4}{5} - \frac{5}{5} = $ ____

**5)** $1\frac{3}{8} - $ ____ $ = \frac{7}{8}$

**6)** ____ $ - \frac{3}{10} = \frac{9}{10}$

What calculations do these number lines show?

**7)**

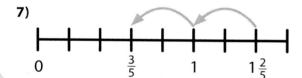

0    $\frac{3}{5}$    1    $1\frac{2}{5}$

**8)**

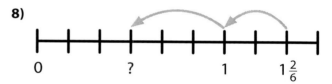

0    ?    1    $1\frac{2}{6}$

## Task **C** (Independent task)

Show the following calculations on a number line:

**1)** $1\frac{3}{8} - \frac{5}{8} - $ ____ $ = \frac{4}{8}$

**2)** $1\frac{2}{9} - \frac{5}{9} = $ ____

**3)** $2\frac{3}{10} - \frac{6}{10} = $ ____

**4)** $1\frac{3}{10} - \frac{1}{2} = $ ____

**5)** $2\frac{1}{7} - $ ____ $ = 1\frac{5}{7}$

**6)** ____ $ - \frac{7}{8} = 1\frac{2}{8}$

**7)** What calculation does this number line show?

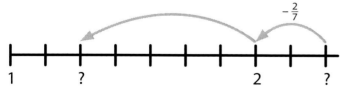

$-\frac{2}{7}$

1    ?    2    ?

**8)** Izzy subtracted $\frac{6}{7}$ on her number line. Her answer was $1\frac{4}{7}$.
What could her calculation be? Try to find more than one answer.

# UNIT 20 Solving problems about adding and subtracting fractions

## National Curriculum link:
Add and subtract fractions with the same denominator.

## Year 4 pupils should already know that:
- It is much easier to calculate with fractions when the denominators are the same
- Finding the difference is another model of subtraction

## Supporting understanding

Children should know that they answer a subtraction calculation by finding the difference between two numbers. The same is true of fractions.

Take the calculation $\frac{9}{10} - \frac{4}{10}$:

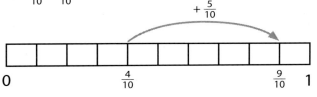

Up to the first vertical line, both fractions are the same.

The difference can easily be seen and can be described in a variety of ways, e.g. $\frac{9}{10}$ is $\frac{5}{10}$ more than $\frac{4}{10}$, the difference between $\frac{9}{10}$ and $\frac{4}{10}$ is $\frac{5}{10}$ or $\frac{4}{10}$ is $\frac{5}{10}$ less than $\frac{9}{10}$.

This can also be shown on a number line by counting up from $\frac{4}{10}$ to $\frac{9}{10}$.

$+\frac{5}{10}$

0     $\frac{4}{10}$     $\frac{9}{10}$   1

## Solving problems

It is important that children have plenty of opportunities to apply knowledge and skills. This not only secures understanding but also provides evidence of learning.

To be successful, children must first make sense of the problem and find a starting point. Children must also decide how best to organise what they do and what they find out.

As teachers, we need to model how to be a problem solver and show children how to organise their thinking.

## In the classroom

Introduce the calculation $\frac{9}{10} - \frac{4}{10}$ using a fraction bar to represent each fraction.

Ask children to describe what is the 'same' and what is 'different':

*In how many different ways can we describe the difference? For example, $\frac{9}{10}$ is $\frac{5}{10}$ more than $\frac{4}{10}$.*

Model this on the number line.

Use different sets of fraction bars for groups to compare, e.g. $\frac{4}{10}$ and $\frac{3}{10}$, $\frac{5}{8}$ and $\frac{3}{8}$, in the same way. (Provide fraction bar resources for groups as needed.)

Encourage children to describe the 'difference' and to create the subtraction calculation in each case.

They should also show the calculation on a number line.

Revisit the calculation $\frac{9}{10} - \frac{4}{10}$ to reinforce that the solution can be found either by finding the difference (as shown) or by subtracting $\frac{4}{10}$ from $\frac{9}{10}$ (model this on the number line).

Introduce the problem that children will be working on during the lesson. It will involve sums and differences, but may also require subtracting amounts to help identify unknown fractions:

*The sum of two fractions is double the difference between them.*

*Is this true for the fractions $\frac{1}{4}$ and $\frac{3}{4}$?*

Ask different groups to find the sum and the difference and to consider the whole problem.

*Now consider these two sets of fractions:*

$\frac{1}{5}$ and $\frac{3}{5}$     $\frac{2}{8}$ and $\frac{6}{8}$

*Is the rule also true for these fractions?*

Ask children to continue to investigate this rule to find out if it is always true, sometimes true or never true.

### ANSWERS
**Task A:** Not true for $\frac{3}{10}$ and $\frac{5}{10}$ or $\frac{1}{5}$ and $\frac{4}{5}$; sometimes true
**Challenge:** $\frac{6}{10}$
**Task B: 1)** $\frac{6}{10}$ **2)** $\frac{1}{6}$ and $\frac{3}{6}$, $\frac{3}{10}$ and $\frac{1}{10}$ or $\frac{3}{10}$ and $\frac{9}{10}$, $\frac{2}{7}$ and $\frac{6}{7}$, $\frac{10}{100}$ and $\frac{30}{100}$, sometimes true **Challenge:** $\frac{4}{10}$ or $3\frac{6}{10}$

**Task C: 1)** E.g. $\frac{1}{6}$ and $\frac{3}{6}$, $\frac{2}{6}$ and $\frac{6}{6}$, $\frac{4}{6}$ and 2; e.g. $\frac{1}{7}$ and $\frac{3}{7}$, $\frac{2}{7}$ and $\frac{6}{7}$, $\frac{4}{7}$ and $1\frac{5}{7}$; e.g. $\frac{1}{10}$ and $\frac{3}{10}$, $\frac{2}{10}$ and $\frac{6}{10}$, $\frac{4}{10}$ and $1\frac{2}{10}$; e.g. $\frac{1}{100}$ and $\frac{3}{100}$, $\frac{10}{100}$ and $\frac{30}{100}$, $\frac{2}{100}$ and $\frac{6}{100}$, $\frac{20}{100}$ and $\frac{60}{100}$, etc; sometimes true; patterns in numerators, i.e. one pair with 3, two pairs with 6, 2, etc.

# Task **A** (Independent task)

The sum of two fractions is double the difference between them.

Is this true for these fractions?

$\frac{1}{6}$ and $\frac{3}{6}$          $\frac{3}{10}$ and $\frac{5}{10}$          $\frac{1}{5}$ and $\frac{4}{5}$          $\frac{1}{10}$ and $\frac{3}{10}$

Now decide if the rule is always true, sometimes true or never true.

**Challenge:**
What fraction can you put with $\frac{2}{10}$ so that the rule is true?

# Task **B** (Independent task)

The sum of two fractions is double the difference between them.

**1)** What fraction can you put with $\frac{2}{10}$ so that the rule is true?

**2)** Can you find a fraction to make the rule true for each of these?

$\frac{1}{6}$          $\frac{3}{10}$          $\frac{2}{7}$          $\frac{10}{100}$

**3)** Now decide if the rule is always true, sometimes true or never true.

**Challenge:** What fraction can you put with $1\frac{2}{10}$ so that the rule is true?

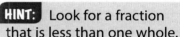

**HINT:** Look for a fraction that is less than one whole.

# Task **C** (Independent task or guided learning with an adult)

The sum of two fractions is double the difference between them.

**1)** Investigate to find pairs of fractions that fit the rule, using:

sixths          sevenths          tenths          hundredths

**2)** Is the rule always true, sometimes true or never true?
What patterns have you noticed?

**HINT:** Fractions can be greater than one whole.

# UNIT 21  Solving problems about fractions

## National Curriculum link:

**Solve simple measure and money problems involving fractions** and decimals to two decimal places.

## Year 4 pupils should already know that:

- Fractions are numbers in their own right
- All fractions can be placed on the number line and some will sit in the same place as others
- Some fractions have the same value but do not look the same, e.g. $\frac{1}{2}$ and $\frac{5}{10}$

## Supporting understanding

In previous units, children have been exploring ordering fractions and finding equivalent fractions.

In this unit, the problem requires children to use this knowledge to help them make decisions when making fractions.

Images like the number line (in a horizontal or vertical orientation) can be used to help order fractions.

Multiplication facts and other images should be used to support children to identify sets of equivalent fractions.

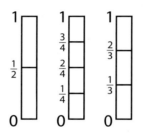

## Solving problems with more than one solution

Children should be encouraged to look for more than one solution and therefore must have access to a range of appropriate problems.

More able children, in particular, can be less inclined to search for additional solutions when one has already been found.

Children should also be challenged with problems where a solution is not possible or where they must look for counterexamples once a rule has been found.

As teachers, we should also model making generalisations and show children how to organise their thinking and results, and consider more than one solution.

**ANSWERS**

**Task A: 1)** Line showing $\frac{1}{3}$ **2)** Pete $\frac{2}{3}$ and Izzy $\frac{9}{10}$ **3)** Pete £10 and Izzy £3 **4)** Pete £20 and Izzy £9

**Task B: 1)** Line showing $\frac{1}{6}$ **2)** Team D $\frac{5}{6}$ and Team E $\frac{7}{10}$ **3)** Team D £10 and Team E £18 **4)** Team D $\frac{4}{6}$ or $\frac{2}{3}$ and Team E $\frac{8}{10}$ or $\frac{4}{5}$ **5)** 0.8

**Task C: 1)** £120 **2)**

|   | After 1 day | | After 2 days | | After 3 days | | After 4 days | | Amount left to reach target | |
|---|---|---|---|---|---|---|---|---|---|---|
| D | $\frac{1}{8}$ | £15 | $\frac{1}{4}$ | £30 | $\frac{3}{5}$ | £72 | $\frac{5}{6}$ | £100 | $\frac{1}{6}$ | £20 |
| E | $\frac{1}{5}$ | £24 | $\frac{3}{10}$ | £36 | $\frac{1}{2}$ | £60 | $\frac{3}{4}$ | £90 | $\frac{1}{4}$ | £30 |
| F | $\frac{1}{6}$ | £20 | $\frac{5}{12}$ | £50 | $\frac{2}{3}$ or $\frac{4}{6}$ | £80 | $\frac{7}{8}$ | £105 | $\frac{1}{8}$ | £15 |

**3)** Line showing $\frac{1}{5}$, $\frac{3}{10}$, $\frac{1}{2}$ and $\frac{3}{4}$ for Team E

## In the classroom

Introduce the problem that will be developed throughout the lesson:

- *Three teams are collecting money for charity.*

- *They are keeping a record of the amount raised so far on a target chart. Here are the results after one week:*

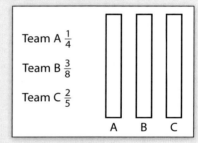

Ask different groups to discuss where lines should be drawn on the bars to show these fractions. Agree and draw on lines.

Pose these, or similar, questions for different groups to consider:

- *How do you know who has collected the most money?*

- *What fraction does each team still need to collect to reach their target? What are these as decimals?*

*At the end of week 2, each team has doubled the amount of money collected.*

- *What fraction has each team collected now?*

- *Who is the closest to reaching their target? How do you know?*

- *If each team collects the same amount in week 3 as they did in week 1, will they have reached their targets? Explain your thinking.*

*The target amount of money for each team is £400.*

- *How much has each team collected at the end of week 1? At the end of week 2? (Team A is the least challenging.)*

# Task **A** (Independent task)

Pete and Izzy are also collecting money for charity.
After day 1 they have collected the following fractions of their target:

Pete: $\frac{1}{3}$        Izzy: $\frac{1}{10}$

**1)** Draw a line on the diagram to show the fraction collected by Pete.

**2)** What fraction do they each still need to collect to reach their target?

**3)** How much money have Pete and Izzy collected so far?

**4)** After day 3, Pete has collected $\frac{2}{3}$ in total and Izzy $\frac{3}{10}$.
How much money do they each have now?

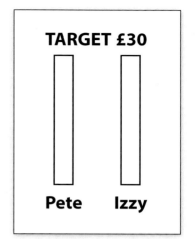

# Task **B** (Independent task)

Teams D and E are also collecting money for charity.
After day 2 they have collected the following fractions of their target:

Team D: $\frac{1}{6}$        Team E: $\frac{3}{10}$

**1)** Draw a line on the diagram to show the fraction collected by Team D.

**2)** What fraction does each team still need to collect to reach their target?

**3)** How much money have each team collected so far?

**4)** After day 5, Team D has collected £40 in total and Team E has collected £48 in total. What fraction has each team collected? Can they be written in another way?

**5)** Write the decimal equivalent for the fraction for Team E.

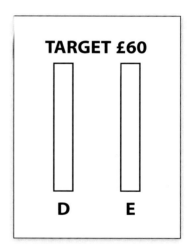

# Task **C** (Independent task or guided learning with an adult)

Teams D, E and F are also collecting money for charity.
The table shows what each team has collected so far:

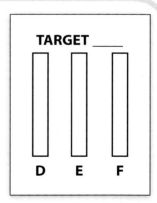

|   | After 1 day | After 2 days | After 3 days | After 4 days | Amount left to reach target | |
|---|---|---|---|---|---|---|
| D | $\frac{1}{8}$ | | £30 | $\frac{3}{5}$ | $\frac{5}{6}$ | $\frac{1}{6}$ | £20 |
| E | $\frac{1}{5}$ | | $\frac{3}{10}$ | £60 | £90 | | £30 |
| F | | £20 | $\frac{5}{12}$ | £80 | $\frac{7}{8}$ | $\frac{1}{8}$ | |

Use the information in the table to:

**1)** Find the target amount of money.        **2)** Fill in the empty boxes in the table.

**3)** Draw a diagram to show the fractions that Team E have collected after 1, 2, 3 and 4 days.

## Problems about fractions and decimals (2)

UNIT 22

### National Curriculum link:
**Solve simple measure and money problems involving fractions and decimals to two decimal places.**

### Year 4 pupils should already know that:
• Decimals and fractions are different ways of expressing numbers and proportions
• All fractions can be shown as decimals using division to help us, e.g. $\frac{1}{2}$ as $1 \div 2 = 0.5$
• Knowing fraction and decimal equivalents is helpful, especially when solving problems

## Supporting understanding

Counting in fraction steps and decimal steps secures understanding of the position of numbers on the number line and the boundaries they sit between.

In this contextualised visual, we can count in tenths (0.1) of a pound, i.e. 10p steps, and then consider other fractions that sit between boundaries:

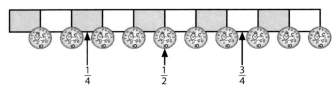

One quarter $\left(\frac{1}{4}\right)$ sits halfway between $\frac{2}{10}$ (0.2) and $\frac{3}{10}$ (0.3) and can be described as $\frac{25}{100}$ or 0.25. This results in the money notation of £0.25.

## Making lists to organise results

In the problem in this unit, we initially know that Abi has $\frac{45}{100}$ of a pound more than Ishmal and that Ishmal has only silver coins.

A table will help to organise possibilities:

| Ishmal | Abi |
|--------|------|
| £0.10 | £0.55 |
| £0.15 | £0.60 |
| £0.20 | £0.65 |
| £0.25 | £0.70 |
| £0.30 | £0.75 |
| etc. | etc. |

As the problem develops, solutions that are no longer possible can be discarded.

**ANSWERS**
**Task A: 1)** $\frac{6}{10}$ **2)** £0.95 and $\frac{95}{100}$ **3)** $\frac{75}{100}$ and $\frac{3}{4}$ **4)** £0.95; Solution 2

**Task B:** Solution 2; Ishmal has a 20p and a 5p coin and Abi has a 50p and two 10p coins or copper coins to the value of 20p

**Task C: 1)** £0.40 or less **2)** See table; the most Asha can have is 50p **3)** Fred £0.61 and Asha £0.45 or Fred £0.62 and Asha £0.45

| Fred | Asha | Sum |
|------|------|------|
| £ 0.51 | £ 0.45 | £ 0.96 |
| £ 0.52 | £ 0.45 | £ 0.97 |
| £ 0.56 | £ 0.45 | £ 1.01 |
| £ 0.57 | £ 0.45 | £ 1.02 |
| £ 0.61 | £ 0.45 | £ 1.06 |
| £ 0.62 | £ 0.45 | £ 1.07 |
| £ 0.51 | £ 0.50 | £ 1.01 |
| £ 0.52 | £ 0.50 | £ 1.02 |
| £ 0.56 | £ 0.50 | £ 1.06 |
| £ 0.57 | £ 0.50 | £ 1.07 |

## In the classroom

Using the image of the counting stick (left), ask children to discuss and explain where these fractions of a pound would be placed, and what their value is in pence and then using £ notation.

$$\frac{1}{2} \qquad \frac{1}{4} \qquad \frac{3}{4} \qquad \frac{3}{5} \qquad \frac{32}{100}$$

Agree positions and values for some of the fractions.

Pose the following problem:

• *Ishmal and Abi each have a fraction of a pound in their pockets. Abi has $\frac{45}{100}$ of a pound more than Ishmal.*

• *Ishmal only has silver coins.*

Ask children to work in groups to suggest possible values in £ notation for Abi and Ishmal. They may choose to use coins if needed.

Pose these, or similar, questions for groups to consider:

• *What do we know about the coins that Abi has?* (They could all be silver.)

• *What is the greatest amount that Ishmal can have? Why?*

Discuss ways to record results. Consider the use of a table to organise solutions.

*Abi has less than $\frac{8}{10}$ of a pound.*

*Ishmal has only two coins, but they are not the same.*

Ask children to consider the solutions that are still possible and those that are not possible, explaining their thinking.

The problem develops in the independent tasks, but note that the build-up to this point of the lesson with children working in groups should be flexible and will take longer than usual.

# Task **A** (Independent task or guided learning with an adult)

We do not know exactly how much money Abi and Ishmal have.

There are three possible solutions:

| Solution | Ishmal | Abi |
|---|---|---|
| 1) | £0.15 | £0.60 |
| 2) | £0.25 | £0.70 |
| 3) | £0.30 | £0.75 |

**1)** How many tenths of a pound does Abi have in Solution 1?

**2)** Add together £0.25 and £0.70 from Solution 2.

Write the amount in pounds (£) and then in hundredths.

**3)** In Solution 3, Abi has £0.75.

Write this amount as two different fractions.

**4)** Abi and Ishmal want to buy a comic between them. It costs £1, but they still need $\frac{5}{100}$ of a pound more. How much money do they have? Which solution is this?

# Task **B** (Independent task)

We still do not know exactly how much money Abi and Ishmal have.

There are three possible solutions now. Use the clues to help find the correct solution and identify the coins they each have.

| Solution | Ishmal | Abi |
|---|---|---|
| 1) | £0.15 | £0.60 |
| 2) | £0.25 | £0.70 |
| 3) | £0.30 | £0.75 |

- The amount in Abi's pocket cannot be written as a fraction in fifths.
- One of Ishmal's coins is worth $\frac{1}{5}$ of a pound.
- One of Abi's coins is worth $\frac{1}{2}$ of a pound.
- Abi does not have any coins that are the same as Ishmal.
- On a number line, Ishmal's amount is halfway between 0.2 and 0.3.

# Task **C** (Independent task or guided learning with an adult)

Fred and Asha each have more than $\frac{2}{5}$ of a pound in their pockets.

**1)** Write down a value that Fred cannot have. Use £ notation.

Here are some other clues to help you:
- The sum of their money is more than $\frac{95}{100}$ of a pound but less than $1\frac{1}{10}$.
- Fred has more money than Asha.
- Asha only has silver coins. Fred also has one copper coin in his pocket.

**2)** Find some possible amounts that they could each have and the sum of their money.

You may find it useful to draw a table.

What is the greatest amount of money that Asha can have?

**3)** Use the next clues to help cross out solutions.
- Fred does not have a coin with a value of £0.05.
- Fred has at least $\frac{1}{10}$ of a pound more than Asha.

What are the possible solutions now?

# RISING ★ STARS

## Maths

# Supporting schools through curriculum change

www.risingstars-uk.com/maths